MONOLINGUAL

THE OXFORD

Picture Dictionary

Canadian Edition

NORMA SHAPIRO AND JAYME ADELSON-GOLDSTEIN

Oxford University Press

Oxford University Press
198 Madison Avenue, New York, NY 10016 USA
Great Clarendon Street, Oxford OX2 6DP England

Oxford University Press Canada
70 Wynford Drive, Don Mills, Ontario M3C 1J9
http://www.oup.com/ca

Oxford New York
Auckland Cape Town Dar es Salaam Hong Kong Karachi
Kuala Lumpur Madrid Melbourne Mexico City Nairobi
New Delhi Shanghai Taipei Toronto
With offices in
Argentina Austria Brazil Chile Czech Republic France Greece
Guatemala Hungary Italy Japan Poland Portugal Singapore
South Korea Switzerland Thailand Turkey Ukraine Vietnam

OXFORD is a trademark of Oxford University Press

Canadian Cataloguing in Publication Data

Shapiro, Norma.
    The Oxford picture dictionary : monolingual

Canadian ed.
Includes index.
ISBN-13: 978 0 19 435270 3
ISBN-10: 0 19 435270 6

1. Picture dictionaries, English. 2. English language-Textbooks
for foreign speakers. I. Adelson-Goldstein, Jayme. II. Title.

PE1629.S49 1999   423'.1   C98-931064-7

Canadian Editorial Consultants: Robert Doyle,
Yvonne MacMillan, Monica Schwalbe
Editorial Manager: Susan Lanzano
Art Director: Lynn Luchetti
Senior Editor: Eliza Jensen
Senior Designer: Susan P. Brorein
Production Layout: David Easter
Production Editor: Klaus Jekeli
Senior Production Editor
(Canadian edition): Robyn F. Clemente
Art Buyer: Tracy A. Hammond
Production Manager: Abram Hall
Pronunciation Editor: Sharon Goldstein
Cover design by Silver Editions

Printing (last digit): 10 9

Printed in Hong Kong

Illustrations by: David Aikins, Doug Archer, Craig Attebery,
Garin Baker, Sally Bensusen, Eliot Bergman, Mark Bischel, Dan
Brown / Artworks NY, Roy Douglas Buchman, George Burgos /
Larry Dodge, Rob Burman, Carl Cassler, Mary Chandler, Robert
Crawford, Dominick D'Andrea, Jim DeLapine, Judy Francis,
Graphic Chart and Map Co., Dale Gustafson, Biruta Akerbergs
Hansen, Marcia Hartsock, C.M.I., David Hildebrand, The Ivy
League of Artists, Inc./ Judy Degraffenreid, The Ivy League of
Artists, Inc. / Tom Powers, The Ivy League of Artists, Inc. / John
Rice, Pam Johnson, Ed Kurtzman, Narda Lebo, Scott A.
MacNeill / MACNEILL & MACINTOSH, Andy Lendway /
Deborah Wolfe Ltd., Jeffrey Mangiat, Karen Minot, Suzanne
Mogensen, Mohammad Mansoor, Tom Newsorn, Melodye
Benson Rosales, Stacey Schuett, Rob Schuster, Don Stewart,
Larry Taugher, Bill Thomson, Anna Veltfort, Nina Wallace,
Wendy Wassink-Ackison, Michael Wepplo, Don Wieland
Thanks to Mike Mikos for his preliminary architectural sketches
of several pieces.

Acknowledgements

The publisher and authors would like to thank the following people for reviewing the manuscript and/or participating in focus groups as the book was being developed:

Ana Maria Aguilera, Lubie Alatriste, Ann Albarelli, Margaret Albers, Sherry Allen, Fiona Armstrong, Ted Auerbach, Steve Austen, Jean Barlow, Sally Bates, Sharon Batson, Myra Baum, Mary Beauparlant, Gretchen Bitterlin, Margrajean Bonilla, Mike Bostwick, Shirley Brod, Lihn Brown, Trish Brys-Overeem, Lynn Bundy, Chris Bunn, Carol Carvel, Leslie Crucil, Jill DeLa Llata, Robert Denheim, Joshua Denk, Kay Devonshire, Thomas Dougherty, Gudrun Draper, Sara Eisen, Lynda Elkins, Ed Ende, Michele Epstein, Beth Fatemi, Andra R. Fawcett, Alice Fiedler, Harriet Fisher, James Fitzgerald, Mary Fitzsimmons, Scott Ford, Barbara Gaines, Elizabeth Garcia Grenados, Maria T. Gerdes, Penny Giacalone, Elliott Glazer, Jill Gluck de la Llata, Javier Gomez, Pura Gonzales, Carole Goodman, Joyce Grabowski, Maggie Grennan, Joanie Griffin, Sally Hansen, Fotini Haritos, Alice Hartley, Fernando Herrera, Ann Hillborn, Mary Hopkins, Lori Howard, Leann Howard, Pamela Howard, Rebecca Hubner, Jan Jarrell, Vicki Johnson, Michele Kagan, Nanette Kafka, Gena Katsaros, Evelyn Kay, Greg Keech, Cliff Ker, Gwen Kerner-Mayer, Marilou Kessler, Patty King, Linda Kiperman, Joyce Klapp, Susan Knutson, Sandy Kobrine, Marinna Kolaitis, Donna Korol, Lorraine Krampe, Karen Kuser, Andrea Lang, Nancy Lebow, Tay Lesley, Gale Lichter, Sandie Linn, Rosario Lorenzano, Louise Louie, Cheryl Lucas, Ronna Magy, Juanita Maltese, Mary Marquardsen, Carmen Marques Rivera, Susan McDowell, Alma McGee, Jerry McLeroy, Kevin McLure, Joan Meier, Patsy Mills, Judy Montague, Vicki Moore, Eneida Morales, Glenn Nadelbach, Elizabeth Neblett, Kathleen Newton, Yvonne Nishio, Afra Nobay, Rosa Elena Ochoa, Jean Owensby, Jim Park, John Perkins, Jane Pers, Laura Peskin, Maria Pick, Percy Pleasant, Selma Porter, Kathy Quinones, Susan Ritter, Martha Robledo, Maureen Rooney, Jean Rose, David Ross, Julietta Ruppert, Lorraine Ruston, Susan Ryan, Frederico Salas, Leslie Salmon, Jim Sandifer, Linda Sasser, Lisa Schreiber, Mary Segovia, Abe Shames, Debra Shaw, Stephanie Shipp, Pat Singh, Mary Sklavos, Donna Stark, Claire Cocoran Stehling, Lynn Sweeden, Joy Tesh, Sue Thompson, Christine Tierney, Laura Topete, Carmen Villanueva, Laura Webber, Renée Weiss, Beth Winningham, Cindy Wislofsky, Judy Wood, Paula Yerman.

A special thanks to Marna Shulberg and the students of the Saticoy Branch of Van Nuys Community Adult School.

We would also like to thank the following individuals and organizations who provided their expertise:

Carl Abato, Alan Goldman, Dr. Larry Falk, Caroll Gray, Henry Haskell, Susan Haskell, Los Angeles Fire Department, Malcolm Loeb, Barbara Lozano, Lorne Dubin, United Farm Workers.

Authors' Acknowledgements

Throughout our careers as English language teachers, we have found inspiration in many places—in the classroom with our remarkable students, at schools, conferences, and workshops with our fellow teachers, and with our colleagues at the ESL Teacher Institute. We are grateful to be part of this international community.

We would like to sincerely thank and acknowledge Eliza Jensen, the project's Senior Editor. Without Eliza, this book would not have been possible. Her indomitable spirit, commitment to clarity, and unwavering advocacy allowed us to realize the book we envisioned.

Creating this dictionary was a collaborative effort and it has been our privilege to work with an exceptionally talented group of individuals who, along with Eliza Jensen, make up the Oxford Picture Dictionary team. We deeply appreciate the contributions of the following people:

Lynn Luchetti, Art Director, whose aesthetic sense and sensibility guided the art direction of this book,

Susan Brorein, Senior Designer, who carefully considered the design of each and every page,

Klaus Jekeli, Production Editor, who pored over both manuscript and art to ensure consistency and accuracy, and

Tracy Hammond, Art Buyer, who skillfully managed thousands of pieces of art and reference material.

We also want to thank Susan Mazer, the talented artist who was by our side for the initial problem-solving and Mary Chandler who also lent her expertise to the project.

We have learned much working with Marjorie Fuchs, Lori Howard, and Renée Weiss, authors of the dictionary's ancillary materials. We thank them for their on-going contributions to the dictionary program.

We must make special mention of Susan Lanzano, Editorial Manager, whose invaluable advice, insights, and queries were an integral part of the writing process.

This book is dedicated to my husband, Neil Reichline, who has encouraged me to take the road less travelled, and to my sons, Eli and Alex, who have allowed me to sit at their baseball games with my yellow notepad. —NS

This book is lovingly dedicated to my husband, Gary and my daughter, Emily Rose, both of whom hugged me tight and let me work into the night. —JAG

A Letter to the Teacher

Welcome to The Oxford Picture Dictionary,
Canadian Edition.

This comprehensive vocabulary resource provides you and your students with over 3,700 words, each defined by engaging art and presented in a meaningful context. *The Oxford Picture Dictionary, Canadian Edition* enables your students to learn and use English in all aspects of their daily lives. The 140 key topics cover home and family, the workplace, the community, health care, and academic studies. The topics are organized into 12 thematic units that are based on the curriculum of beginning and low-intermediate level English language coursework. The word lists of the dictionary include both single word entries and verb phrases. Many of the prepositions and adjectives are presented in phrases as well, demonstrating the natural use of words in conjunction with one another.

The Oxford Picture Dictionary, Canadian Edition uses a variety of visual formats, each suited to the topic being represented. Where appropriate, word lists are categorized and pages are divided into sections, allowing you to focus your students' attention on one aspect of a topic at a time.

Within the word lists:

- nouns, adjectives, prepositions, and adverbs are numbered,

- verbs are bolded and identified by letters, and

- targeted prepositions and adjectives within phrases are bolded.

The dictionary includes a variety of exercises and self access tools that will guide your students towards accurate and fluent use of the new words.

- Exercises at the bottom of the pages provide vocabulary development through pattern practice, application of the new language to other topics, and personalization questions.

- An alphabetical index assists students in locating all words and topics in the dictionary.

- A phonetic listing for each word in the index and a pronunciation guide give students the key to accurate pronunciation.

- A verb index of all the verbs presented in the dictionary provides students with information on the present, past, and past participle forms of the verbs.

The Oxford Picture Dictionary, Canadian Edition is the core of *The Oxford Picture Dictionary Program* which includes a *Teacher's Book* and its companion *Focused* *Listening Cassette, Beginning* and *Intermediate Workbooks, Classic Classroom Activities* (a photocopiable activity book), *Overhead Transparencies,* and *Read All About It 1* and *2.*

TEACHING THE VOCABULARY

Your students' needs and your own teaching philosophy will dictate how you use *The Oxford Picture Dictionary, Canadian Edition* with your students. The following general guidelines, however, may help you adapt the dictionary's pages to your particular course and students. (For topic-specific, step-by-step guidelines and activities for presenting and practising the vocabulary on each dictionary page see the *Oxford Picture Dictionary Teacher's Book.*)

Preview the topic

A good way to begin any lesson is to talk with students to determine what they already know about the topic. Some different ways to do this are:

- Ask general questions related to the topic;

- Have students brainstorm a list of words they know from the topic; or

- Ask questions about the picture(s) on the page.

Present the vocabulary

Once you've discovered which words your students already know, you are ready to focus on presenting the words they need. Introducing 10–15 new words in a lesson allows students to really learn the new words. On pages where the word lists are longer, and students are unfamiliar with many of the words, you may wish to introduce the words by categories or sections, or simply choose the words you want in the lesson.

Here are four different presentation techniques. The techniques you choose will depend on the topic being studied and the level of your students.

- Say each new word and describe or define it within the context of the picture.

- Demonstrate verbs or verb sequences for the students, and have volunteers demonstrate the actions as you say them.

- Use Total Physical Response commands to build comprehension of the vocabulary: *Put the pencil on your book. Put it on your notebook. Put it on your desk.*

- Ask a series of questions to build comprehension and give students an opportunity to say the new words:

▶ Begin with *yes/no* questions. *Is #16 chalk?* (yes)

▶ Progress to *or* questions. *Is #16 chalk or a marker?* (chalk)

▶ Finally, ask *Wh* questions.

What can I use to write on this paper? (a marker/ Use a marker.)

Check comprehension

Before moving on to the practice stage, it is helpful to be sure all students understand the target vocabulary. There are many different things you can do to check students' understanding. Here are two activities to try:

• Tell students to open their books and point to the items they hear you say. Call out target vocabulary at random as you walk around the room checking to see if students are pointing to the correct pictures.

• Make true/false statements about the target vocabulary. Have students hold up two fingers for true, three fingers for false. *You can write with a marker.* [two fingers] *You raise your notebook to talk to the teacher.* [three fingers]

Take a moment to review any words with which students are having difficulty before beginning the practice activities.

Practise the vocabulary

Guided practice activities give your students an opportunity to use the new vocabulary in meaningful communication. The exercises at the bottom of the pages are one source of guided practice activities.

• **Talk about...** This activity gives students an opportunity to practise the target vocabulary through sentence substitutions with meaningful topics.

e.g. **Talk about your feelings.**

I feel <u>happy</u> when I see my friends.

• **Practise...** This activity gives students practice using the vocabulary within common conversational functions such as making introductions, ordering food, making requests, etc.

e.g. **Practise asking for things in the dining room.**

Please pass <u>the platter</u>.

May I have <u>the creamer</u>?

Could I have <u>a fork</u>, please?

• **Use the new language.** This activity asks students to brainstorm words within various categories, or may

ask them to apply what they have learned to another topic in the dictionary. For example, on *Colours*, page 12, students are asked to look at *Clothing I*, pages 64–65, and name the colours of the clothing they see.

• **Share your answers.** These questions provide students with an opportunity to expand their use of the target vocabulary in personalized discussion. Students can ask and answer these questions in whole class discussions, pair or group work, or they can write the answers as journal entries.

Further guided and communicative practice can be found in the *Oxford Picture Dictionary Teacher's Book* and in *Classic Classroom Activities*. The *Oxford Picture Dictionary Beginning* and *Intermediate Workbooks* and *Read All About It 1* and *2* provide your students with controlled and communicative reading and writing practice.

We encourage you to adapt the materials to suit the needs of your classes.

Jayme Adelson-Goldstein

Norma Shapiro

A Letter to the Student

Dear Student of English,

Welcome to *The Oxford Picture Dictionary, Canadian Edition.* The more than 3,700 words in this book will help you as you study English.

Each page in this dictionary teaches about a specific topic. The topics are grouped together in units. All pages in a unit have the same colour and symbol. For example, each page in the Food unit has this symbol:

On each page you will see pictures and words. The pictures have numbers or letters that match the numbers or letters in the word lists. Verbs (action words) are identified by letters and all other words are identified by numbers.

How to find words in this book

- Use the Table of Contents, pages vii–ix.
  Look up the general topic you want to learn about.

- Use the Index, pages 173–205.
  Look up individual words in alphabetical (A–Z) order.

- Go topic by topic.
  Look through the book until you find something that interests you.

How to use the Index

When you look for a word in the index this is what you will see:

the word   the number (or letter) in the word list

apples [ăp/əlz] **50**–4

the pronunciation   the page number

If the word is on one of the maps, pages 122–125, you will find it in the Geographical Index on pages 206–208.

How to use the Verb Guide

When you want to know the past form of a verb or its past participle form, look up the verb in the verb guide. The regular verbs and their spelling changes are listed on pages 170–171. The simple form, past form, and past participle form of irregular verbs are listed on page 172.

Workbooks

There are two workbooks to help you practise the new words:
The Oxford Picture Dictionary Beginning and *Intermediate Workbooks, Canadian Editions.*

As authors and teachers we both know how difficult English can be (and we're native speakers!). When we wrote this book, we asked teachers and students for their help and ideas. We hope their ideas and ours will help you.

We wish you success!

Jayme Adelson-Goldstein   *Norma Shapiro*

Contents

1. Everyday Language

2. People

3. Housing

4. Food

Contents

Contents

10. Plants and Animals

11. Work

12. Recreation

A Classroom

1. chalkboard/blackboard **3.** student **5.** teacher **7.** chair/seat

2. screen **4.** overhead projector **6.** desk

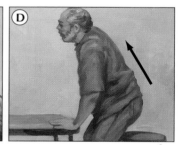

A. Raise your hand.

B. Talk to the teacher.

C. Listen to a cassette.

D. Stand up.

E. Sit down./Take a seat.

F. Point to the picture.

G. Write on the board.

H. Erase the board.

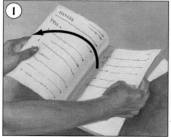

I. Open your book.

J. Close your book.

K. Take out your pencil.

L. Put away your pencil.

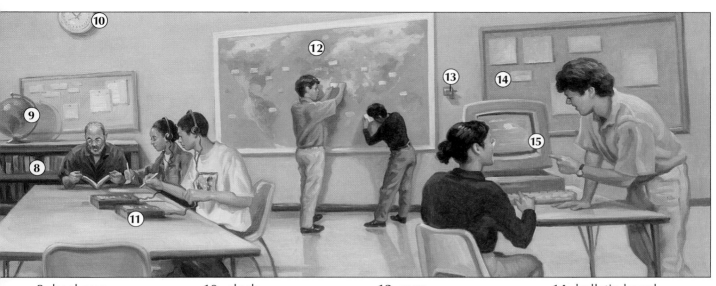

8. bookcase	**10.** clock	**12.** map	**14.** bulletin board
9. globe	**11.** cassette player	**13.** pencil sharpener	**15.** computer

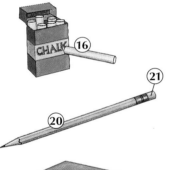

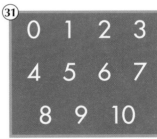

16. chalk	**20.** pencil	**24.** binder	**28.** dictionary
17. chalkboard/ blackboard eraser	**21.** pencil eraser	**25.** loose leaf paper	**29.** picture dictionary
	22. textbook	**26.** spiral notebook	**30.** the alphabet
18. pen	**23.** workbook	**27.** ruler	**31.** numbers
19. marker			

Use the new language.

1. Name three things you can open.

2. Name three things you can put away.

3. Name three things you can write with.

Share your answers.

1. Do you like to raise your hand?

2. Do you ever listen to cassettes in class?

3. Do you ever write on the board?

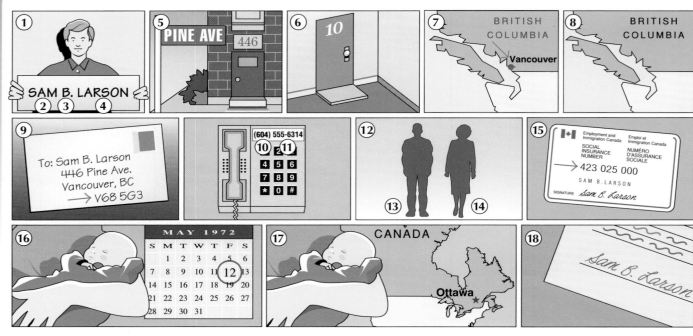

(1) SAM B. LARSON **(2)(3)(4)**

(5) PINE AVE 446

(6) 10

(7) BRITISH COLUMBIA → Vancouver

(8) BRITISH COLUMBIA

(9) To: Sam B. Larson / 446 Pine Ave. / Vancouver, BC → V6B 5G3

(10)(11) (604) 555-6314

(12)(13)(14)

(15) Employment and Immigration Canada / Emploi et Immigration Canada / SOCIAL INSURANCE NUMBER / NUMÉRO D'ASSURANCE SOCIALE → 423 025 000 / SAM B. LARSON / SIGNATURE Sam B. Larson

(16) MAY 1972 — S M T W T F S / 1 2 3 4 5 6 / 7 8 9 10 11 12 13 / 14 15 16 17 18 19 20 / 21 22 23 24 25 26 27 / 28 29 30 31

(17) CANADA / Ottawa

(18) Sam B. Larson

School Registration Form

1. name _____

    2. first name   **3.** middle initial   **4.** last name

5. address _____   **6.** apt. # * _____

7. city _____   **8.** province/territory _____   **9.** postal code _____

  (   )
_____   _____ – _____ – _____

10. area code   **11.** telephone number   **12.** sex: **13.** ☐ male   **15.** Social Insurance number

                       14. ☐ female

16. date of birth _____   **17.** place of birth _____
         (month) (date) (year)

*apt. # = apartment number   **18.** signature _____

(A) L-A-R-S-O-N

A. Spell your name.

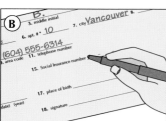

(B) 3. middle initial B. / 6. apt. # 10 / 7. city Vancouver 8. / (604) 555-6314 11. telephone number / 8. area code / 15. Social Insurance number / 17. place of birth / date) (year) / 18. signature

B. Fill out a form.

(C) SAM B. LARSON

C. Print your name.

(D) Sam B. Larson

D. Sign your name.

Talk about yourself.

My first name is Sam.
My last name is spelled L-A-R-S-O-N.
I come from Ottawa.

Share your answers.

1. Do you like your first name?
2. Is your last name from your mother? father? husband?
3. What is your middle name?

1. classroom	**7.** lockers	**13.** principal's office
2. teacher	**8.** washrooms	**14.** principal
3. auditorium	**9.** gym	**15.** counsellor's office
4. cafeteria	**10.** bleachers	**16.** counsellor
5. lunch benches	**11.** track	**17.** main office
6. library	**12.** field	**18.** administrative assistant

More vocabulary

instructor: teacher

coach: gym teacher

administrator: principal or other school supervisor

Share your answers.

1. Do you ever talk to the principal of your school?
2. Is there a place for you to eat at your school?
3. Does your school look the same as or different from the one in the picture?

Studying

Dictionary work

A. **Look up** a word.

B. **Read** the word.

C. **Say** the word.

D. **Repeat** the word.

E. **Spell** the word.

F. **Copy** the word.

Work with a partner

G. **Ask** a question.

H. **Answer** a question.

I. **Share** a book.

J. **Help** your partner.

Work in a group

K. **Brainstorm** a list.

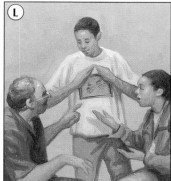

L. **Discuss** the list.

M. **Draw** a picture.

N. **Dictate** a sentence.

Class work

O. Pass out the papers.

P. Talk with each other.

Q. Collect the papers.

Follow directions

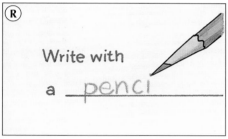

Write with

a _pencil_

R. Fill in the blank.

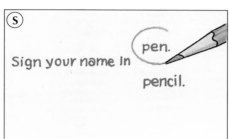

Sign your name in (pen.)

pencil.

S. Circle the answer.

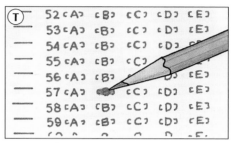

| 52 cAɔ cBɔ cCɔ cDɔ cEɔ |
| 53 cAɔ cBɔ cCɔ cDɔ cEɔ |
| 54 cAɔ cBɔ cCɔ cDɔ cEɔ |
| 55 cAɔ cBɔ cCɔ |
| 56 cAɔ cBɔ cDɔ cEɔ |
| 57 cAɔ cCɔ cDɔ cEɔ |
| 58 cAɔ cBɔ cCɔ cDɔ cEɔ |
| 59 cAɔ cBɔ cCɔ cDɔ cEɔ |

T. Mark the answer sheet.

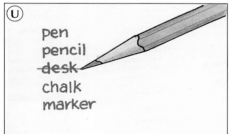

pen
pencil
~~desk~~
chalk
marker

U. Cross out the word.

Give me the pencil.

V. Underline the word.

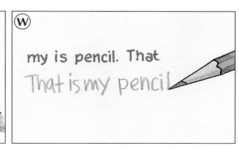

my is pencil. That

That is my pencil

W. Put the words **in order.**

1. sit   ___ a. pencil
2. write   ___ b. book
3. read   ___ c. chair

X. Match the items.

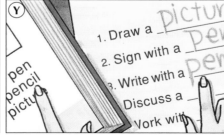

1. Draw a _pictur_
2. Sign with a _pen_
3. Write with a _pen_
Discuss a ___
Work with ___

pen
pencil
pictu

Y. Check your work.

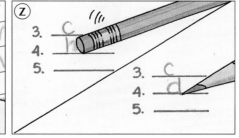

3. _c_
4.
5.

3. _c_
4. _d_
5.

Z. Correct the mistake.

Share your answers.

1. Do you like to work in groups?
2. Do you like to share books?
3. Do you like to answer questions?

4. Is it easy for you to talk with your classmates?
5. Do you always check your work?
6. Do you cross out your mistakes or erase them?

A. greet someone

B. begin a conversation   **C. end** the conversation

D. introduce yourself   **E. make sure** you **understand**   **F. introduce** your friend

G. compliment your friend   **H. thank** your friend   **I. apologize**

Practise introductions.

Hi, I'm <u>Sam Jones</u> and this is my friend, <u>Pat Green</u>.

  Nice to meet you. I'm <u>Tomas Garcia</u>.

Practise giving compliments.

That's a great <u>sweater</u>, <u>Tomas</u>.

  Thanks <u>Pat</u>. I like your <u>shoes</u>.

Look at **Clothing I,** pages **64–65** for more ideas.

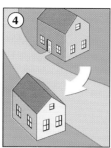

Operator.

What city please?
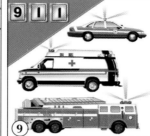

1. telephone / phone

2. receiver

3. cord

4. local call

5. long-distance call

6. international call

7. operator

8. directory assistance (411)

9. emergency service (911)

10. phone card / calling card

11. pay phone

12. cordless phone

13. cellular phone / cellphone

14. answering machine

15. telephone book / phone book

16. pager

Using a pay phone

A. **Pick up** the receiver.

B. **Listen** for the dial tone.

C. **Deposit** coins.

D. **Dial** the number.

E. **Leave** a message.

F. **Hang up** the receiver.

More vocabulary

When you get a person or place that you didn't want to call, we say you have the **wrong number.**

Share your answers.

1. What kinds of calls do you make?

2. How much does it cost to call your country?

3. Do you like to talk on the telephone?

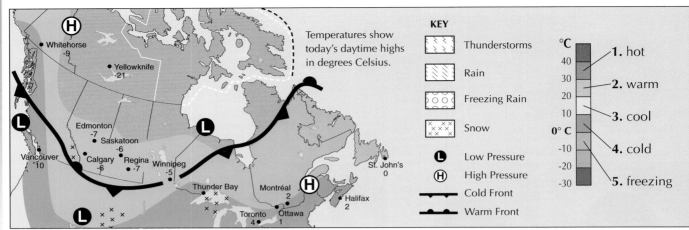

Temperatures show today's daytime highs in degrees Celsius.

KEY

(pattern)	Thunderstorms
(pattern)	Rain
(pattern)	Freezing Rain
(pattern)	Snow
L	Low Pressure
H	High Pressure
▼▼	Cold Front
●●	Warm Front

°C
40 — 1. hot
30 — 2. warm
20
10 — 3. cool
0° C
-10 — 4. cold
-20
-30 — 5. freezing

Whitehorse -9
Yellowknife -21
Edmonton -7
Saskatoon -6
Calgary -6
Regina -7
Winnipeg -5
Vancouver -10
Thunder Bay
Montréal 2
Toronto 4
Ottawa 1
Halifax 2
St. John's 0

6. sunny/clear   **7.** cloudy   **8.** raining   **9.** snowing

10. windy	**13.** icy	**16.** thunderstorm	**19.** hail
11. foggy	**14.** smoggy	**17.** lightning	**20.** snowstorm
12. humid	**15.** heat wave	**18.** hailstorm	**21.** dust storm

---

Language note: *it is, there is*

For **1–14** we use,   *It's cloudy.*

For **15–21** we use,   *There's a heat wave.*
                       There's lightning.

Talk about the weather.

Today it's hot. It's 32 degrees.
Yesterday it was warm. It was 25 degrees.

1. **little** hand

2. **big** hand

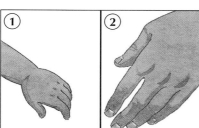

13. **heavy** box

14. **light** box

3. **fast** driver

4. **slow** driver

15. **neat** closet

16. **messy** closet

5. **hard** chair

6. **soft** chair

17. **good** dog

18. **bad** dog

7. **thick** book/
fat book

8. **thin** book

19. **expensive** ring

20. **cheap** ring

9. **full** glass

10. **empty** glass

21. **beautiful** view

22. **ugly** view

11. **noisy** children/
loud children

12. **quiet** children

23. **easy** problem

24. **difficult** problem/
hard problem

$3+2=X$ $\dfrac{x^2-x}{12}=1$

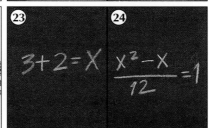

Use the new language.
1. Name three things that are thick.
2. Name three things that are soft.
3. Name three things that are heavy.

Share your answers.
1. Are you a slow driver or a fast driver?
2. Do you have a neat closet or a messy closet?
3. Do you like loud or quiet parties?

Colours

1. blue	**6.** orange	**11.** brown
2. dark blue	**7.** purple	**12.** yellow
3. light blue	**8.** green	**13.** red
4. turquoise	**9.** beige	**14.** white
5. grey	**10.** pink	**15.** black

Use the new language.
Look at **Clothing I,** pages **64–65.**
Name the colours of the clothing you see.
That's a dark blue suit.

Share your answers.
1. What colours are you wearing today?
2. What colours do you like?
3. Is there a colour you don't like? What is it?

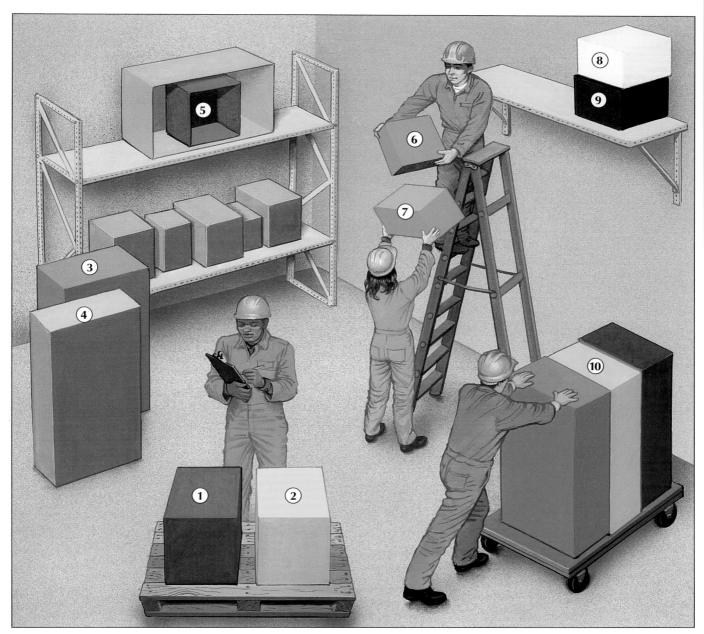

1. The red box is **next to** the yellow box, **on the left.**

2. The yellow box is **next to** the red box, **on the right.**

3. The turquoise box is **behind** the grey box.

4. The grey box is **in front of** the turquoise box.

5. The dark blue box is **in** the beige box.

6. The green box is **above** the orange box.

7. The orange box is **below** the green box.

8. The white box is **on** the black box.

9. The black box is **under** the white box.

10. The pink box is **between** the purple box and the brown box.

More vocabulary

near: in the same area
*The white box is **near** the black box.*

far from: not near
*The red box is **far from** the black box.*

Numbers and Measurements

| HOME | 1 8 |
| VISITOR | 2 2 |

CALGARY
235 Kilometres

Cardinals

0 zero	11 eleven	21 twenty-one	101 one hundred and one
1 one	12 twelve	22 twenty-two	1000 one thousand
2 two	13 thirteen	30 thirty	1001 one thousand and one
3 three	14 fourteen	40 forty	10 000 ten thousand
4 four	15 fifteen	50 fifty	100 000 one hundred thousand
5 five	16 sixteen	60 sixty	1 000 000 one million
6 six	17 seventeen	70 seventy	1 000 000 000 one billion
7 seven	18 eighteen	80 eighty	
8 eight	19 nineteen	90 ninety	
9 nine	20 twenty	100 one hundred	
10 ten			

Ordinals

1st first	8th eighth	15th fifteenth
2nd second	9th ninth	16th sixteenth
3rd third	10th tenth	17th seventeenth
4th fourth	11th eleventh	18th eighteenth
5th fifth	12th twelfth	19th nineteenth
6th sixth	13th thirteenth	20th twentieth
7th seventh	14th fourteenth	

Roman numerals

I	= 1	VII	= 7	XXX	= 30
II	= 2	VIII	= 8	XL	= 40
III	= 3	IX	= 9	L	= 50
IV	= 4	X	= 10	C	= 100
V	= 5	XV	= 15	D	= 500
VI	= 6	XX	= 20	M	= 1000

Fractions

1. 1/8   one-eighth

2. 1/4   one-quarter /
one-fourth

3. 1/3   one-third

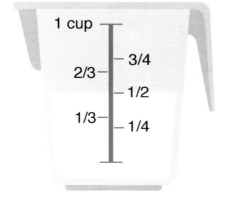

1 cup

3/4

2/3

1/2

1/3

1/4

4. 1/2   one-half

5. 3/4   three-quarters /
three-fourths

6. 1   whole

Per Cents

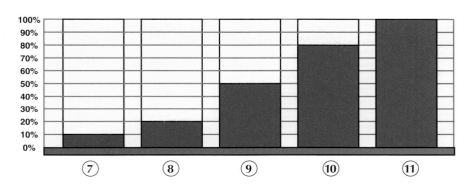

⑦   ⑧   ⑨   ⑩   ⑪

7. 10%   ten per cent

8. 20%   twenty per cent

9. 50%   fifty per cent

10. 80%   eighty per cent

11. 100%   one hundred per cent

Measurement

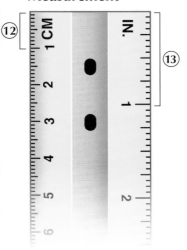

12. centimetre [cm]
13. inch [in.]

Units of measure

Length: millimetre (mm),
centimetre (cm), metre (m),
kilometre (km)

Area: square centimetre (cm²),
square metre (m²), hectare
(ha), square kilometre (km²)

Volume: millilitre (mL), litre (L),
cubic centimetre (cm³),
cubic metre (m³)

Mass: milligram (mg),
gram (g), kilogram (kg),
tonne (t)

Speed: kilometres per hour
(km/h), metres per second
(m/s)

Dimensions

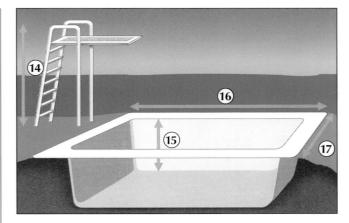

14. height

15. depth

16. length

17. width

More vocabulary

measure: to find the size or amount of something
count: to find the total number of something

Share your answers.

1. How many students are in class today?
2. Who was the first person in class today?
3. How far is it from your home to your school?

Time

1. second

2. minute **3.** hour

A.M.

P.M.

4. 1:00
one o'clock

5. 1:05
one-oh-five
five after one

6. 1:10
one-ten
ten after one

7. 1:15
one-fifteen
a quarter after one

8. 1:20
one-twenty
twenty after one

9. 1:25
one twenty-five
twenty-five after one

10. 1:30
one-thirty
half past one

11. 1:35
one thirty-five
twenty-five to two

12. 1:40
one-forty
twenty to two

13. 1:45
one forty-five
a quarter to two

14. 1:50
one-fifty
ten to two

15. 1:55
one fifty-five
five to two

Talk about the time.

What time is it? It's <u>10:00 a.m.</u>

What time do you wake up on weekdays? At <u>6:30 a.m.</u>

What time do you wake up on weekends? At <u>9:30 a.m.</u>

Share your answers.

1. How many hours a day do you study English?

2. You are meeting friends at 1:00. How long will you wait for them if they are late?

16

16. morning

17. noon

18. afternoon

19. evening

20. night

21. midnight

22. early

23. late

TIME ZONES

24. Hawaii-Aleutian time

25. Alaska time

26. Pacific time

27. Mountain time

28. Central time

29. Eastern time

30. Atlantic time

31. Newfoundland time

32. Standard time

33. daylight saving time

More vocabulary

on time: not early and not late

*He's **on time.***

Share your answers.

1. When do you watch television? study? do housework?

2. Do you come to class on time? early? late?

Days of the week

1. Sunday

2. Monday

3. Tuesday

4. Wednesday

5. Thursday

6. Friday

7. Saturday

8. year

9. month

10. day

11. week

12. weekdays

13. weekend

14. date

15. today

16. tomorrow

17. yesterday

18. last week

19. this week

20. next week

21. every day

22. once a week

23. twice a week

24. three times a week

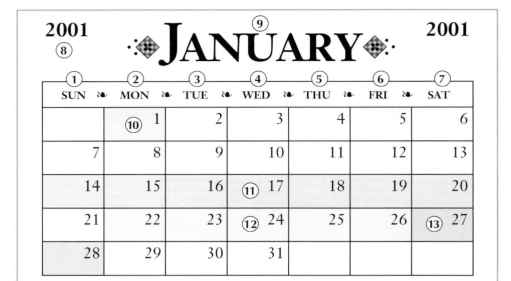

Talk about the calendar.

What's today's date? It's <u>May 10th</u>.

What day is it? It's <u>Tuesday</u>.

What day was yesterday? It was <u>Monday</u>.

Share your answers.

1. How often do you come to school?

2. How long have you been in this school?

2001

JAN (25)
SUN	MON	TUE	WED	THU	FRI	SAT
	1	2	3	4	5	6
7	8	9	10	11	12	13
14	15	16	17	18	19	20
21	22	23	24	25	26	27
28	29	30	31			

FEB (26)
SUN	MON	TUE	WED	THU	FRI	SAT
				1	2	3
4	5	6	7	8	9	10
11	12	13	14	15	16	17
18	19	20	21	22	23	24
25	26	27	28			

MAR (27)
SUN	MON	TUE	WED	THU	FRI	SAT
				1	2	3
4	5	6	7	8	9	10
11	12	13	14	15	16	17
18	19	20	21	22	23	24
25	26	27	28	29	30	31

APR (28)
SUN	MON	TUE	WED	THU	FRI	SAT
1	2	3	4	5	6	7
8	9	10	11	12	13	14
15	16	17	18	19	20	21
22	23	24	25	26	27	28
29	30					

MAY (29)
SUN	MON	TUE	WED	THU	FRI	SAT
		1	2	3	4	5
6	7	8	9	10	11	12
13	14	15	16	17	18	19
20	21	22	23	24	25	26
27	28	29	30	31		

JUN (30)
SUN	MON	TUE	WED	THU	FRI	SAT
					1	2
3	4	5	6	7	8	9
10	11	12	13	14	15	16
17	18	19	20	21	22	23
24	25	26	27	28	29	30

JUL (31)
SUN	MON	TUE	WED	THU	FRI	SAT
1	2	3	4	5	6	7
8	9	10	11	12	13	14
15	16	17	18	19	20	21
22	23	24	25	26	27	28
29	30	31				

AUG (32)
SUN	MON	TUE	WED	THU	FRI	SAT
			1	2	3	4
5	6	7	8	9	10	11
12	13	14	15	16	17	18
19	20	21	22	23	24	25
26	27	28	29	30	31	

SEP (33)
SUN	MON	TUE	WED	THU	FRI	SAT
						1
2	3	4	5	6	7	8
9	10	11	12	13	14	15
16	17	18	19	20	21	22
23/30	24	25	26	27	28	29

OCT (34)
SUN	MON	TUE	WED	THU	FRI	SAT
	1	2	3	4	5	6
7	8	9	10	11	12	13
14	15	16	17	18	19	20
21	22	23	24	25	26	27
28	29	30	31			

NOV (35)
SUN	MON	TUE	WED	THU	FRI	SAT
				1	2	3
4	5	6	7	8	9	10
11	12	13	14	15	16	17
18	19	20	21	22	23	24
25	26	27	28	29	30	

DEC (36)
SUN	MON	TUE	WED	THU	FRI	SAT
						1
2	3	4	5	6	7	8
9	10	11	12	13	14	15
16	17	18	19	20	21	22
23/30	24/31	25	26	27	28	29

MARCH 21

JUNE 21

SEPT. 21

DEC. 21

JUNE 5 — TIM!

MARCH 2 — ANNIVERSARY

JULY 1 — CANADA DAY — CITY BANK — CLOSED-JULY1

APRIL 4 — EASTER SUNDAY

MAY 17 — DOCTOR 4:30

AUGUST

Months of the year

25. January

26. February

27. March

28. April

29. May

30. June

31. July

32. August

33. September

34. October

35. November

36. December

Seasons

37. spring

38. summer

39. fall

40. winter

41. birthday

42. anniversary

43. statutory holiday

44. religious holiday

45. appointment

46. vacation

Use the new language.

Look at the **ordinal numbers** on page **14**.
Use ordinal numbers to say the date.
It's June 5th. It's the fifth.

Talk about your birthday.

My birthday is in the winter.
My birthday is in January.
My birthday is on January twenty-sixth.

Money

Coins

1. $.01 = 1¢
a penny/1 cent

2. $.05 = 5¢
a nickel/5 cents

3. $.10 = 10¢
a dime/10 cents

4. $.25 = 25¢
a quarter/25 cents

5. $1.00
a loonie/a dollar

6. $2.00
a toonie/two dollars

Bills

7. $5.00
five dollars

8. $10.00
ten dollars

9. $20.00
twenty dollars

10. $50.00
fifty dollars

11. $100.00
one hundred dollars

Ways to pay

12. cash

13. personal cheque

14. credit card

15. money order

16. traveller's cheque

More vocabulary

borrow: to get money from someone and return it later
lend: to give money to someone and get it back later
pay back: to return the money that you borrowed

Other ways to talk about money:

a five-dollar bill or *a five*
a ten-dollar bill or *a ten*

a twenty-dollar bill or *a twenty*

A. shop for	**E. keep**	**2.** regular price	**6.** price/cost
B. sell	**F. return**	**3.** sale price	**7.** sales tax
C. pay for/**buy**	**G. exchange**	**4.** bar code	**8.** total
D. give	**1.** price tag	**5.** receipt	**9.** change

More vocabulary

When you use a credit card to shop, you get a **bill** in the mail. Bills list, in writing, the items you bought and the total you have to pay.

Share your answers.

1. Name three things you pay for every month.
2. Name one thing you will buy this week.
3. Where do you like to shop?

Age and Physical Description

1. children
2. baby
3. toddler

4. 6-year-old boy
5. 10-year-old girl
6. teenagers

7. 13-year-old boy
8. 19-year-old girl
9. adults

10. woman
11. man
12. senior citizen

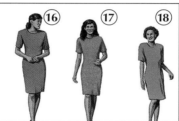

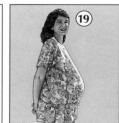

13. young
14. middle-aged
15. elderly
16. tall

17. average height
18. short
19. pregnant
20. heavyset

21. average weight
22. thin/slim
23. attractive
24. cute

25. physically challenged
26. visually impaired
27. hearing impaired

Talk about yourself and your teacher.
I am <u>young</u>, <u>average height</u>, and <u>average weight</u>.
My teacher is <u>a middle-aged</u>, <u>tall</u>, <u>thin</u> man.

Use the new language.
Turn to **Hobbies and Games**, pages **162–163**.
Describe each person on the page.
He's <u>a heavyset</u>, <u>short</u>, <u>senior citizen</u>.

1. short hair	**8.** bangs	**15.** black hair	**22.** comb
2. shoulder-length hair	**9.** straight hair	**16.** blond hair	**A. cut** hair
3. long hair	**10.** wavy hair	**17.** brown hair	**B. perm** hair
4. part	**11.** curly hair	**18.** brush	**C. set** hair
5. moustache	**12.** bald	**19.** scissors	**D. colour** hair / **dye** hair
6. beard	**13.** grey hair	**20.** blow dryer	
7. sideburns	**14.** red hair	**21.** rollers / curlers	

More vocabulary

hair stylist: a person who cuts, sets, and perms hair
hair salon: the place where a hair stylist works

Talk about your hair.

My hair is long, straight, and brown.
I have long, straight, brown hair.
When I was a child my hair was short, curly, and blond.

Family

Tom Lee's Family

1. grandparents

Min

Lu

2. grandmother
3. grandfather

4. parents

Rose

Chang

Helen

Daniel

5. mother
6. father

10. aunt
11. uncle

Tom

Lily

Alex

Emily

8. sister
9. brother

12. cousin

7. (Min and Lu's) grandson

Berta

Mario

Ana Garcia's Family

13. mother-in-law
14. father-in-law

Ana

Marta

Carlos

Tito

20. (Tito's) wife

15. sister-in-law
16. brother-in-law

19. husband

Alice

Eddie

Sara

Felix

17. niece
18. nephew

21. daughter
22. son

More vocabulary

Lily and Emily are Min and Lu's **granddaughters.**

Daniel is Min and Lu's **son-in-law.**

Ana is Berta and Mario's **daughter-in-law.**

Share your answers.

1. How many brothers and sisters do you have?
2. What number son or daughter are you?
3. Do you have any children?

24

Lisa Smith's Family

23. married

Carol   Dan

Lisa

24. divorced

25. single mother

26. single father

27. remarried

Rick   Carol

Dan   Sue

Rick   Carol

28. stepfather

David

29. half brother

Mary

30. half sister

Lisa

Dan   Sue

31. stepmother

Kim   Bill

32. stepsister   **33.** stepbrother

More vocabulary

Carol is Dan's **former wife**.

Sue is Dan's **wife**.

Dan is Carol's **former husband**.

Rick is Carol's **husband**.

Lisa is the **stepdaughter** of both Rick and Sue.

Daily Routines

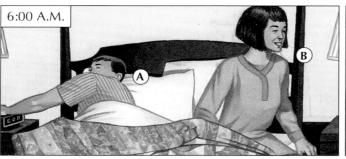

A. **wake up**

B. **get up**

C. **have / take** a shower

D. **get dressed**

E. **eat** breakfast

F. **make** lunch

G. **take** the children to school

H. **take** the bus to school

I. **drive** to work / **go** to work

J. **be** in school

K. **work**

L. **go** to the grocery store /
do the grocery shopping

M. **leave** work

Grammar point: 3rd person singular
For **he** and **she**, we add **-s** or **-es** to the verb.
He/She wakes up.
He/She watches TV.

These verbs are different (irregular):
be   *He/She is in school at 10:00 a.m.*
have   *He/She has dinner at 6:30 p.m.*

5:30 P.M.  **N** **O**	6:00 P.M.  **P** **Q**
6:30 P.M.  **R**	7:30 P.M.  **S** **T**
8:00 P.M.  **U** **V**	8:30 P.M.  **W**
10:30 P.M.  **X**	11:00 P.M. 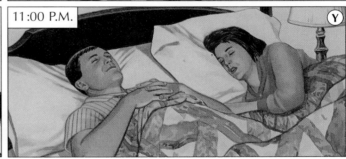 **Y**

N. clean the house

O. pick up the children

P. cook dinner / supper

Q. come home / **get** home

R. have dinner / supper

S. watch TV

T. do homework

U. relax

V. read the paper

W. exercise

X. go to bed

Y. go to sleep

Talk about your daily routine.

I take a shower in the morning.

I go to school in the evening.

I go to bed at 11 o'clock.

Share your answers.

1. Who makes dinner / supper in your family?

2. Who does the grocery shopping?

3. Who goes to work?

Life Events

A. **be born**

B. **start** school

C. **immigrate**

D. **graduate**

E. **learn** to drive

F. **join** the army

G. **get** a job

H. **become** a citizen

I. **rent** an apartment

J. **go** to college/university

K. **fall in love**

L. **get married**

Grammar point: past tense

start			immigrate		be — was
learn			graduate		get — got
join	+ed		move	+d	become — became
rent			retire		go — went
travel	double the final consonant +ed (travelled)		die		fall — fell

These verbs are different (irregular):

be	— was	have	— had
get	— got	buy	— bought
become	— became		
go	— went		
fall	— fell		

 1960

M. **have** a baby

 1967

N. **travel**

 1971

O. **buy** a house

 1971

P. **move**

 1985

Q. **have** a grandchild

 1997

R. **die**

 1

1. birth certificate

 2

2. diploma

 3

3. Record of Landing

 4

4. driver's licence

 5

5. Social Insurance card

 6

6. Certificate of Canadian Citizenship

 7

7. university degree

 8

8. marriage licence

 9

9. passport

More vocabulary

When a husband dies, his wife becomes a **widow**.
When a wife dies, her husband becomes a **widower**.
When older people stop working, we say they **retire**.

Talk about yourself.

I was born in 1968.
I learned to drive in 1987.
I immigrated in 1990.

Feelings

1. hot

2. thirsty

3. sleepy

4. cold

5. hungry

6. full

7. comfortable

8. uncomfortable

9. disgusted

10. calm

11. nervous

12. in pain

13. worried

14. sick

15. well

16. relieved

17. hurt

18. lonely

19. in love

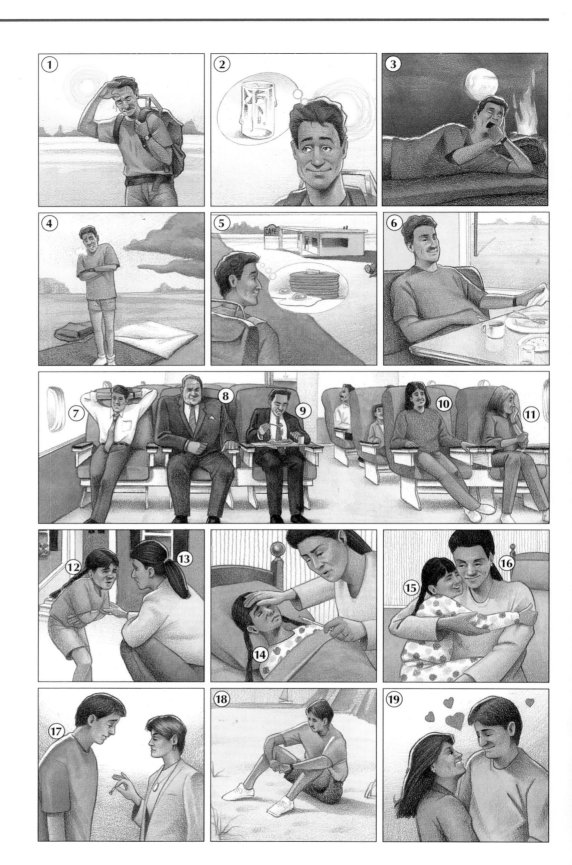

More vocabulary

furious: very angry

terrified: very scared

overjoyed: very happy

exhausted: very tired

starving: very hungry

humiliated: very embarrassed

Talk about your feelings.

I feel <u>happy</u> when I see <u>my friends</u>.

I feel <u>homesick</u> when I think about <u>my family</u>.

20. sad

21. homesick

22. proud

23. excited

24. scared

25. embarrassed

26. bored

27. confused

28. frustrated

29. angry

30. upset

31. surprised

32. happy

33. tired

Use the new language.

Look at **Clothing I,** page **64,** and answer the questions.

1. How does the runner feel?

2. How does the man at the bus stop feel?

3. How does the woman at the bus stop feel?

4. How do the teenagers feel?

5. How does the little boy feel?

The Ceremony

1. graduating class	**5.** podium	**9.** guest speaker	**B. applaud / clap**
2. gown	**6.** graduate	**10.** audience	**C. cry**
3. cap	**7.** diploma	**11.** photographer	**D. take** a picture
4. stage	**8.** valedictorian	**A. graduate**	**E. give** a speech

Talk about what the people in the pictures are doing.

She is
⎡ tak**ing** a picture.
│ giv**ing** a speech.
│ smil**ing**.
⎣ laugh**ing**.

He is
⎡ mak**ing** a toast.
⎣ clap**ping**.

They are
⎡ graduat**ing**.
│ hug**ging**.
│ kiss**ing**.
⎣ applaud**ing**.

12. caterer	**15.** banner	**18.** gifts	**H.** laugh
13. buffet	**16.** dance floor	**F.** kiss	**I.** make a toast
14. guests	**17.** DJ (disc jockey)	**G.** hug	**J.** dance

Share your answers.

1. Did you ever go to a graduation? Whose?
2. Did you ever give a speech? Where?
3. Did you ever hear a great speaker? Where?

4. Did you ever go to a graduation party?
5. What do you like to eat at parties?
6. Do you like to dance at parties?

Places to Live

1. the city/an urban area   **2.** the suburbs   **3.** a small town   **4.** the country/a rural area

5. apartment building

6. house

7. townhouse

8. semi-detached house

9. university residence

10. shelter

11. nursing home

12. ranch

13. farm

More vocabulary

duplex house: a house divided into two homes

condominium: an apartment building where each apartment is owned separately

co-op: an apartment building owned by the residents

Share your answers.

1. Do you like where you live?
2. Where did you live in your country?
3. What types of housing are there near your school?

34

Renting an apartment

A. look for a new apartment

B. talk to the manager/superintendent

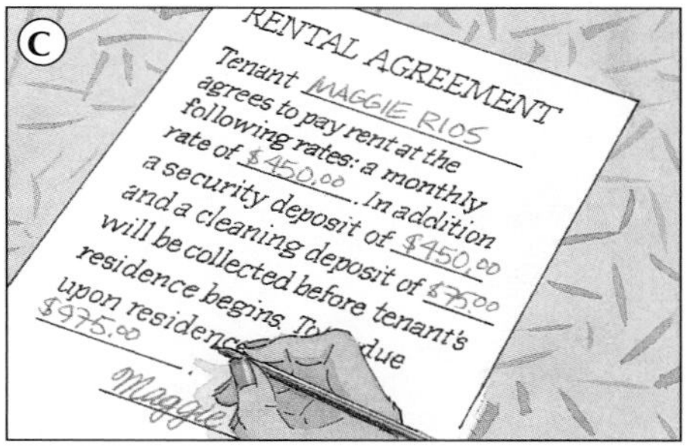

C. sign a rental agreement

D. move in

E. unpack

F. pay the rent

Buying a house

G. talk to the real estate agent

H. make an offer

I. get a loan

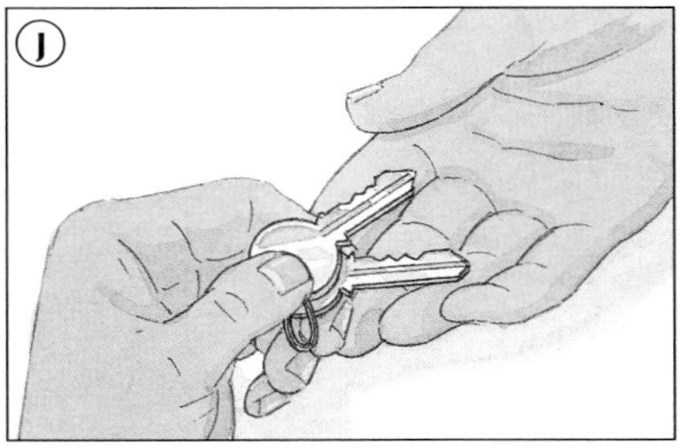

J. take ownership

K. arrange the furniture

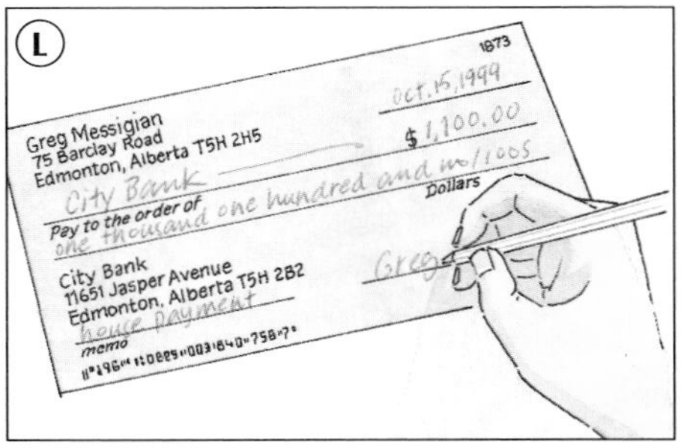

L. pay the mortgage

More vocabulary

lease: a rental agreement for a specific period of time

utilities: gas, water, and electricity for the home

Practise talking to an apartment manager/superintendent.

How much is the rent?

Are utilities included?

When can I move in?

Apartments

Entrance

Laundry Room

Recreation Room

Garage

1. first floor

2. second floor

3. third floor

4. fourth floor

5. roof garden

6. playground

7. fire escape

8. intercom / speaker

9. security system

10. doorman

11. vacancy sign

12. manager / superintendent

13. security gate

14. storage locker

15. parking space

More vocabulary

rec room: a short way of saying **recreation room**

basement: the area below the street level of an apartment or a house

Talk about where you live.

I live in _Apartment 3 near the entrance._

I live in _Apartment 11 on the second floor near the fire escape._

Hallway

FIRE EXIT

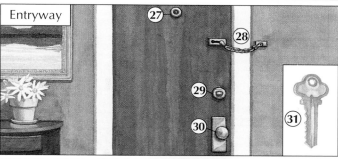

Entryway

Office

Lobby

16. swimming pool	**23.** fire exit	**30.** doorknob
17. balcony	**24.** garbage chute	**31.** key
18. courtyard	**25.** smoke detector	**32.** landlord
19. air conditioner	**26.** stairway	**33.** tenant
20. garbage bin	**27.** peephole	**34.** elevator
21. alley/lane	**28.** door chain	**35.** stairs
22. neighbour	**29.** deadbolt lock	**36.** mailboxes

Grammar point: *there is, there are*

singular: *there is*   plural: *there are*

There is a fire exit in the hallway.

There are mailboxes in the lobby.

Talk about apartments.

My apartment has an elevator, a lobby, and a rec room.

My apartment doesn't have a pool or a garage.

My apartment needs air conditioning.

A House

1. floor plan
2. backyard
3. fence
4. mailbox
5. driveway
6. garage

7. garage door
8. screen door
9. porch light
10. doorbell
11. front door
12. storm door

13. steps
14. front walk
15. front yard
16. deck
17. window
18. shutter

19. eavestrough
20. roof
21. chimney
22. TV antenna

More vocabulary
two-storey house: a house with two floors
downstairs: the bottom floor
upstairs: the part of a house above the bottom floor

Share your answers.
1. What do you like about this house?
2. What's something you don't like about the house?
3. Describe the perfect house.

1. hedge	**8.** sprinkler	**15.** pruning shears	**22.** lawn mower
2. hammock	**9.** hose	**16.** wheelbarrow	**A.** **weed** the flower bed
3. garbage can	**10.** compost pile	**17.** watering can	**B.** **water** the plants
4. leaf blower	**11.** rake	**18.** flowerpot	**C.** **mow** the lawn
5. patio furniture	**12.** hedge clippers	**19.** flower	**D.** **plant** a tree
6. patio	**13.** shovel	**20.** bush	**E.** **trim** the hedge
7. barbecue	**14.** trowel	**21.** lawn	**F.** **rake** the leaves

Talk about your yard and gardening.

I like to plant trees.

I don't like to weed.

I like/don't like to work in the yard/garden.

Share your answers.

1. What flowers, trees, or plants do you see in the picture? (Look at **Trees, Plants, and Flowers,** pages **128–129** for help.)

2. Do you ever use a barbecue to cook?

A Kitchen

1. cabinet/cupboard	**8.** shelf	**15.** toaster oven	**22.** counter
2. paper towels	**9.** refrigerator	**16.** pot	**23.** drawer
3. dish drainer/dish rack	**10.** freezer	**17.** kettle	**24.** pan
4. dishwasher	**11.** coffee maker	**18.** stove	**25.** electric mixer
5. garburator	**12.** blender	**19.** burner/element	**26.** food processor
6. sink	**13.** microwave oven	**20.** oven	**27.** cutting board
7. toaster	**14.** electric can opener	**21.** oven drawer	

Talk about the location of kitchen items.

The toaster oven is *on the counter* *near the stove*.

The microwave is *above the stove*.

Share your answers.

1. Do you have a garburator? a dishwasher? a microwave?

2. Do you eat in the kitchen?

1. china cabinet	**8.** candlestick	**15.** pepper shaker	**22.** knife
2. set of dishes	**9.** vase	**16.** dining room chair	**23.** spoon
3. platter	**10.** tray	**17.** dining room table	**24.** plate
4. ceiling fan	**11.** teapot	**18.** tablecloth	**25.** bowl
5. light fixture	**12.** sugar bowl	**19.** napkin/serviette	**26.** glass
6. serving dish	**13.** creamer	**20.** placemat	**27.** cup
7. candle	**14.** salt shaker	**21.** fork	**28.** mug

Practise asking for things in the dining room.

Please pass <u>the platter</u>.

May I have <u>the creamer</u>?

Could I have <u>a fork</u>, please?

Share your answers.

1. What are the women in the picture saying?

2. In your home, where do you eat?

3. Do you like to make dinner for your friends?

A Living Room

1. bookcase	**8.** mantel	**15.** floor lamp	**22.** magazine holder
2. basket	**9.** fireplace	**16.** drapes	**23.** coffee table
3. track lighting	**10.** fire	**17.** window	**24.** armchair/easy chair
4. lightbulb	**11.** fire screen	**18.** plant	**25.** love seat
5. ceiling	**12.** logs	**19.** sofa/couch/chesterfield	**26.** TV (television)
6. wall	**13.** wall unit	**20.** throw pillow	**27.** carpet
7. painting	**14.** stereo system	**21.** end table	

Use the new language.

Look at **Colours,** page **12,** and describe this room.

There is a grey sofa and a grey armchair.

Talk about your living room.

In my living room I have a sofa, two chairs, and a coffee table.

I don't have a fireplace or a wall unit.

1. hamper	**8.** towel rack	**15.** toilet paper	**22.** sink
2. bathtub	**9.** tile	**16.** toilet brush	**23.** soap
3. rubber mat	**10.** shower head	**17.** toilet	**24.** soap dish
4. drain	**11.** (mini)blinds	**18.** mirror	**25.** wastebasket
5. hot water	**12.** bath towel	**19.** medicine cabinet	**26.** scale
6. faucet/tap	**13.** hand towel	**20.** toothbrush	**27.** bath mat
7. cold water	**14.** washcloth/face cloth	**21.** toothbrush holder	

More vocabulary

half bath: a bathroom without a shower or bathtub
linen closet: a closet or cabinet for towels and sheets
shower stall: a shower without a bathtub

Share your answers.

1. Do you turn off the water when you brush your teeth? wash your hair? shave?

2. Does your bathroom have a bathtub or a shower stall?

A Bedroom

1. mirror

2. dresser/bureau/ chest of drawers

3. drawer

4. closet

5. curtains

6. window shade/blind

7. photograph

8. bed

9. pillow

10. pillowcase

11. bedspread

12. blanket

13. flat sheet

14. fitted sheet

15. headboard

16. clock radio

17. lamp

18. lampshade

19. light switch

20. outlet

21. night table

22. dust ruffle/bedskirt

23. rug

24. floor

25. mattress

26. box spring

27. bed frame

Use the new language.
Describe this room. (See **Describing Things**, page **11**, for help.)
I see a soft pillow and a beautiful bedspread.

Share your answers.
1. What is your favourite thing in your bedroom?
2. Do you have a clock in your bedroom? Where is it?
3. Do you have a mirror in your bedroom? Where is it?

1. bunk bed	**7.** bumper pad	**13.** diaper pail	**19.** cradle
2. comforter	**8.** chest of drawers	**14.** dollhouse	**20.** colouring book
3. night light	**9.** baby monitor	**15.** blocks	**21.** crayons
4. mobile	**10.** teddy bear	**16.** ball	**22.** puzzle
5. wallpaper	**11.** smoke detector	**17.** picture book	**23.** stuffed animals
6. crib	**12.** change table	**18.** doll	**24.** toy chest

Talk about where items are in the room.

The dollhouse is near *the colouring book*.
The teddy bear is on *the chest of drawers*.

Share your answers.

1. Do you think this is a good room for children? Why?
2. What toys did you play with when you were a child?
3. What children's stories do you know?

A. **dust** the furniture

B. **recycle** the newspapers

C. **clean** the oven

D. **wash** the windows

E. **sweep** the floor

F. **empty** the wastebasket

G. **make** the bed

H. **put away** the toys

I. **vacuum** the carpet

J. **mop** the floor

K. **polish** the furniture

L. **scrub** the floor

M. **wash** the dishes

N. **dry** the dishes

O. **wipe** the counter

P. **change** the sheets

Q. **take out** the garbage

Talk about yourself.

I wash the dishes every day.

I change the sheets every week.

I never dry the dishes.

Share your answers.

1. Who does the housework in your family?

2. What is your favourite cleaning job?

3. What is your least favourite cleaning job?

1. feather duster	**9.** squeegee	**17.** dust mop
2. recycling bin	**10.** broom	**18.** furniture polish
3. oven cleaner	**11.** dustpan	**19.** scrub brush
4. rubber gloves	**12.** garbage bags	**20.** bucket/pail
5. steel-wool soap pads	**13.** vacuum cleaner	**21.** dishwashing liquid/dish soap
6. rags	**14.** vacuum cleaner attachments	**22.** dish towel/tea towel
7. stepladder	**15.** vacuum cleaner bag	**23.** cleanser
8. glass cleaner	**16.** (wet)mop	**24.** sponge

Practise asking for the items.

I want to <u>wash the windows</u>.
Please hand me <u>the squeegee</u>.

I have to <u>sweep the floor</u>.
Can you get me <u>the broom</u>, please?

Household Problems and Repairs

1. The water heater is **not working**.

2. The power is **out**.

3. The roof is **leaking**.

4. The wall is **cracked**.

5. The window is **broken**.

6. The lock is **broken**.

7. The steps are **broken**.

8. roofer

9. electrician

10. repair person

11. locksmith

12. carpenter

13. fuse box

14. gas meter

Use the new language.
Look at **Tools and Building Supplies,** pages **150–151.**
Name the tools you use for household repairs.

I use <u>a hammer and nails</u> to fix <u>a broken step</u>.
I use <u>a wrench</u> to repair <u>a dripping tap</u>.

15. The furnace is **broken**.

16. The tap is **dripping**.

17. The sink is **overflowing**.

18. The toilet is **plugged**.

19. The pipes are **frozen**.

20. plumber

21. exterminator

Household pests

22. termite(s)

23. flea(s)

24. ant(s)

25. cockroach(es)

26. mice*

27. rat(s)

*Note: *one mouse, two mice*

More vocabulary

fix: to repair something that is broken

exterminate: to kill household pests

pesticide: a chemical that is used to kill household pests

Share your answers.

1. Who does household repairs in your home?
2. What is the worst problem a home can have?
3. What is the most expensive problem a home can have?

Fruit

1. grapes	**9.** grapefruit	**17.** strawberries	**25.** dates
2. pineapples	**10.** oranges	**18.** raspberries	**26.** prunes
3. bananas	**11.** lemons	**19.** blueberries	**27.** raisins
4. apples	**12.** limes	**20.** papayas	**28.** not ripe
5. peaches	**13.** tangerines	**21.** mangoes	**29.** ripe
6. pears	**14.** avocados	**22.** coconuts	**30.** over ripe
7. apricots	**15.** cantaloupes	**23.** nuts	
8. plums	**16.** cherries	**24.** watermelons	

Language note: *a bunch of*
We say *a bunch of grapes* and *a bunch of bananas.*

Share your answers.
1. Which fruits do you put in a fruit salad?
2. Which fruits are sold in your area in the summer?
3. What fruits did you have in your country?

1. lettuce	**9.** celery	**17.** green onions/scallions	**25.** green beans/ string beans
2. cabbage	**10.** parsley	**18.** eggplants	**26.** mushrooms
3. carrots	**11.** spinach	**19.** peas	**27.** corn
4. zucchini	**12.** cucumbers	**20.** artichokes	**28.** onions
5. radishes	**13.** squash	**21.** potatoes	**29.** garlic
6. beets	**14.** turnips	**22.** sweet potatoes/yams	
7. green peppers	**15.** broccoli	**23.** tomatoes	
8. chili peppers	**16.** cauliflower	**24.** asparagus	

Language note: *a bunch of, a head of*

We say *a bunch of carrots, a bunch of celery,* and *a bunch of spinach.*

We say *a head of lettuce, a head of cabbage,* and *a head of cauliflower.*

Share your answers.

1. Which vegetables do you eat raw? cooked?

2. Which vegetables need to be in the refrigerator?

3. Which vegetables don't need to be in the refrigerator?

Meat and Poultry

Beef

1. beef roast
2. steak
3. stewing beef
4. ground beef

5. beef ribs
6. veal cutlets
7. liver
8. tripe

Pork

9. ham
10. pork chops
11. bacon
12. sausage

Lamb

13. lamb shanks
14. leg of lamb
15. lamb chops

16. chicken
17. turkey
18. duck

19. breasts
20. wings
21. thighs

22. drumsticks
23. gizzards

24. **raw** chicken
25. **cooked** chicken

More vocabulary

vegetarian: a person who doesn't eat meat
Meat and poultry without bones are called **boneless**.
Poultry without skin is called **skinless**.

Share your answers.

1. What kind of meat do you eat most often?
2. What kind of meat do you use in soup?
3. What part of the chicken do you like the most?

DELI

1. white bread	**6.** pastrami	**11.** Swiss cheese
2. brown / whole wheat bread	**7.** roast beef	**12.** mozzarella cheese
3. rye bread	**8.** corned beef	**13.** potato salad
4. smoked turkey	**9.** processed cheese	**14.** coleslaw
5. salami	**10.** cheddar cheese	**15.** pasta salad

SEAFOOD

Fish

16. trout	**20.** halibut
17. catfish	**21.** filet of sole
18. whole salmon	
19. salmon steak	

Shellfish

22. crab	**26.** mussels
23. lobster	**27.** oysters
24. shrimp	**28.** clams
25. scallops	**29. fresh** fish
	30. frozen fish

Practise ordering a sandwich.

I'd like <u>roast beef</u> and <u>cheddar cheese</u> on <u>rye bread</u>.

Tell what you want on it.

Please put <u>tomato</u>, <u>lettuce</u>, <u>onions</u>, and <u>mustard</u> on it.

Share your answers.

1. Do you like to eat fish?
2. Do you buy fresh or frozen fish?

The Supermarket

1. bottle return
2. meat and poultry section

3. shopping cart
4. canned goods
5. aisle

6. baked goods
7. shopping basket
8. manager

9. dairy section
10. pet food
11. produce section

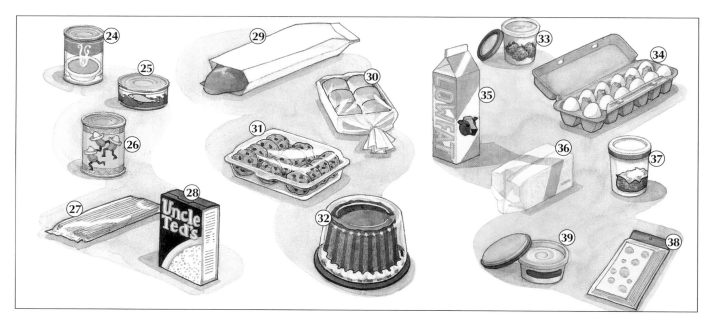

24. soup
25. tuna
26. beans
27. spaghetti

28. rice
29. bread
30. rolls
31. cookies

32. cake
33. yogurt
34. eggs
35. milk

36. butter
37. sour cream
38. cheese
39. margarine

12. frozen foods	**15.** beverages	**18.** cash register	**21.** bagger
13. baking products	**16.** snack foods	**19.** cashier	**22.** paper bag
14. paper products	**17.** checkout/cash	**20.** line	**23.** plastic bag

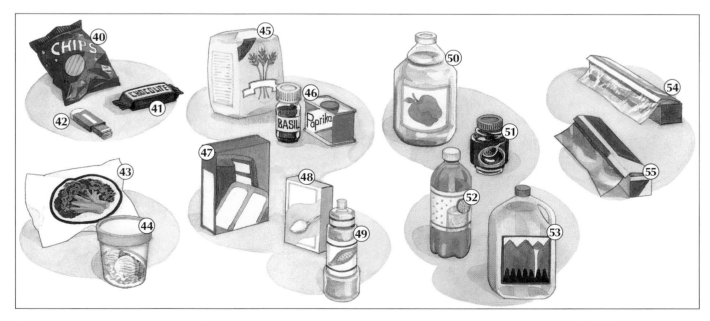

40. potato chips	**44.** ice cream	**48.** sugar	**52.** soft drink/pop
41. candy bar/ chocolate bar	**45.** flour	**49.** oil	**53.** bottled water
42. gum	**46.** herbs and spices	**50.** apple juice	**54.** plastic wrap
43. frozen vegetables	**47.** cake mix	**51.** instant coffee	**55.** aluminum foil/tin foil

Containers and Packaged Foods

1. bottle

2. jar

3. can

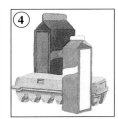
4. carton

5. container

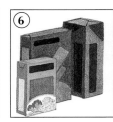
6. box

7. bag

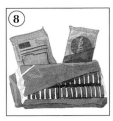
8. package

9. six-pack

10. loaf

11. roll

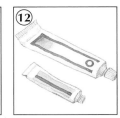
12. tube

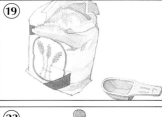

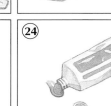

13. a bottle of pop

14. a jar of jam

15. a can of soup

16. a carton of eggs

17. a container of cottage cheese

18. a box of cereal

19. a bag of flour

20. a package of cookies

21. a six-pack of pop

22. a loaf of bread

23. a roll of paper towels

24. a tube of toothpaste

Grammar point: *How much? How many?*
Some foods can be counted: *one apple, two apples.*
How many *apples do you need? I need* ***two*** *apples.*

Some foods cannot be counted, like liquids, grains, spices, or dairy foods. For these, count containers: *one box of rice, two boxes of rice.*
How much *rice do you need? I need* ***two boxes.***

A. Measure the ingredients.

B. Weigh the food.

1 cup = 237 millilitres

C. Convert the measurements.

Liquid measures

(1) 1 cup →
237 mL / 1c.

(2) Mayonnaise
500 mL

(3) Frozen YOGURT
2 L

(4) MILK
1 L

(5)
4 L

Dry measures

(6)
5 mL / 1 tsp.

(7) Sugar
15 mL / 1 tbsp.

(8) Brown Sugar
60 mL / 1/4 c.

(9)
118 mL / 1/2 c.

(10) FLOUR
237 mL / 1 c.

Weight

(11)
.500 kg

(12)
1.00 kg

1. a cup of oil

2. a 500-mL jar of mayonnaise

3. a 2-litre container of yogurt

4. a litre of milk

5. a 4-litre jug of apple juice

6. 5 mL or a teaspoon of salt

7. 15 mL or a tablespoon of sugar

8. 60 mL or a 1/4 cup of brown sugar

9. 118 mL or a 1/2 cup of raisins

10. 237 mL or a cup of flour

11. 500 grams of cheese

12. a kilo(gram) of beef

More vocabulary:

recipe: directions for preparing a food

ingredients: items that go into preparing a food

Share your answers.

1. What do you like to bake?

2. What baked goods are popular in your country?

3. What are the main ingredients?

Food Preparation

Scrambled eggs

A. **Break** 3 eggs.

B. **Beat** well.

C. **Grease** the pan.

D. **Pour** the eggs into the pan.

E. **Stir.**

F. **Cook** until done.

Vegetable casserole

G. **Chop** the onions.

H. **Sauté** the onions.

I. **Steam** the broccoli.

J. **Grate** the cheese.

K. **Mix** the ingredients.

L. **Bake** at 350° for 45 minutes.

Chicken soup

M. **Cut up** the chicken.

N. **Peel** the carrots.

O. **Slice** the carrots.

P. **Boil** the chicken.

Q. **Add** the vegetables.

R. **Simmer** for 1 hour.

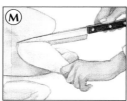  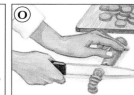

Five ways to cook chicken

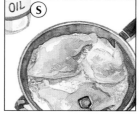   

S. fry   T. barbecue   U. roast   V. broil   W. stir-fry

Talk about the way you prepare these foods.

I *fry* eggs.

I *bake* potatoes.

Share your answers.

1. What are popular ways in your country to make rice? vegetables? meat?

2. What is your favourite way to cook chicken?

1. can opener

2. grater

3. plastic storage container

4. steamer

5. frying pan

6. pot

7. ladle

8. double boiler

9. wooden spoon

10. garlic press

11. casserole dish

12. carving knife

13. roasting pan

14. roasting rack

15. vegetable peeler

16. paring knife

17. colander

18. kitchen timer

19. spatula

20. egg beater

21. whisk

22. strainer

23. tongs

24. lid

25. saucepan

26. cake pan

27. cookie sheet

28. pie plate

29. pot holders

30. rolling pin

31. mixing bowl

Talk about how to use the utensils.

You use a peeler to peel potatoes.

You use a pot to cook soup.

Use the new language.

Look at **Food Preparation, page 58.**

Name the different utensils you see.

Fast Food

1. hamburger	**8.** green salad	**15.** doughnut	**22.** sweetener
2. french fries/chips	**9.** taco	**16.** salad bar	**23.** ketchup
3. cheeseburger	**10.** nachos	**17.** lettuce	**24.** mustard
4. pop	**11.** frozen yogurt	**18.** salad dressing	**25.** mayonnaise
5. iced tea	**12.** milkshake	**19.** booth	**26.** relish
6. hot dog	**13.** counter	**20.** straw	**A.** **eat**
7. pizza	**14.** muffin	**21.** sugar	**B.** **drink**

More vocabulary
donut: doughnut (spelling variation)
condiments: relish, mustard, ketchup, mayonnaise, etc.

Share your answers.
1. What would you order at this restaurant?
2. Which fast foods are popular in your country?
3. How often do you eat fast food? Why?

Breakfast

Lunch

Dinner

Desserts

Beverages

1. scrambled eggs

2. sausage

3. toast

4. waffles

5. syrup

6. pancakes

7. bacon

8. grilled cheese sandwich

9. chef's salad

10. soup of the day

11. mashed potatoes

12. roast chicken

13. steak

14. baked potato

15. pasta

16. garlic bread

17. fried fish

18. rice pilaf

19. cake

20. pudding

21. pie

22. coffee

23. decaf coffee

24. tea

Practise ordering from the menu.

I'd like a grilled cheese sandwich and some soup.

I'll have the chef's salad and a cup of decaf coffee.

Use the new language.

Look at **Fruit,** page **50.**

Order a slice of pie using the different fruit flavours.

Please give me a slice of apple pie.

A Restaurant

1. hostess

2. dining room

3. menu

4. server/waiter

5. patron/diner

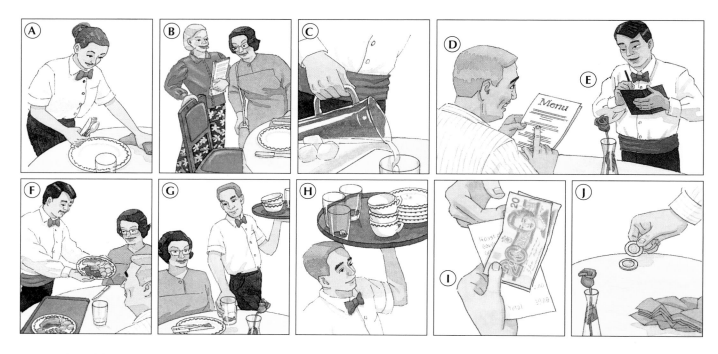

A. set the table

B. seat the customer

C. pour the water

D. order from the menu

E. take the order

F. serve the meal

G. clear the table

H. carry the tray

I. pay the bill

J. leave a tip

More vocabulary

eat out: to go to a restaurant to eat

take out: to buy food at a restaurant and take it home to eat

Practise giving commands.

Please <u>set the table</u>.

I'd like you to <u>clear the table</u>.

It's time to <u>serve the meal</u>.

6. server / waitress   **8.** bread basket   **10.** kitchen   **12.** dishroom

7. dessert tray   **9.** busperson   **11.** chef   **13.** dishwasher

 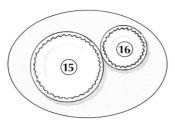  

  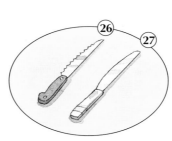 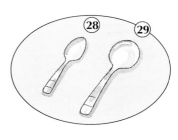

14. place setting   **18.** soup bowl   **22.** saucer   **26.** steak knife

15. dinner plate   **19.** water glass   **23.** napkin / serviette   **27.** knife

16. bread-and-butter plate   **20.** wine glass   **24.** salad fork   **28.** teaspoon

17. salad plate   **21.** cup   **25.** dinner fork   **29.** soup spoon

Talk about how you set the table in your home.

The glass is on the right.
The fork goes on the left.
The napkin is next to the plate.

Share your answers.

1. Do you know anyone who works in a restaurant? What does he or she do?

2. In your opinion, which restaurant jobs are hard? Why?

Clothing I

1. three-piece suit

2. suit

3. dress

4. shirt

5. jeans

6. sports coat/sports jacket

7. turtleneck

8. slacks/pants

9. blouse

10. skirt

11. pullover

12. T-shirt

13. shorts

14. sweatshirt

15. sweatpants

More vocabulary:

outfit: clothes that look nice together

When clothes are popular, they are **in fashion.**

Talk about what you're wearing today and what you wore yesterday.

I'm wearing <u>a grey sweater</u>, <u>a red T-shirt</u>, and <u>blue jeans</u>.

Yesterday I wore <u>a green pullover</u>, <u>a white shirt</u>, and <u>black slacks</u>.

16. coveralls	**21.** overalls	**26.** sports shirt
17. uniform	**22.** tunic	**27.** cardigan
18. jumper	**23.** leggings	**28.** tuxedo
19. maternity dress	**24.** vest	**29.** evening gown
20. golf shirt	**25.** split skirt / culottes	

Use the new language.
Look at **A Graduation,** pages **32–33.**
Name the clothes you see.
The man at the podium is wearing a suit.

Share your answers.
1. Which clothes in this picture are in fashion now?
2. Who is the best-dressed person in this line? Why?
3. What do you wear when you go to the movies?

1. hat	**5.** gloves
2. overcoat	**6.** cap
3. leather jacket	**7.** jacket
4. wool scarf/muffler	

8. parka	**12.** earmuffs
9. mittens	**13.** down vest
10. toque	**14.** ski mask/balaclava
11. tights	**15.** down jacket

16. umbrella	**20.** trench coat
17. raincoat	**21.** sunglasses
18. poncho	**22.** swimming trunks
19. rain boots	**23.** straw hat

24. windbreaker
25. cover-up
26. swimsuit/bathing suit
27. baseball cap

Use the new language.
Look at **Weather,** page **10.**
Name the clothing for each weather condition.
Wear a windbreaker when it's windy.

Share your answers.
1. Which is better in the rain, an umbrella or a poncho?
2. Which is better in the cold, a parka or a down jacket?
3. Do you have more summer clothes or winter clothes?

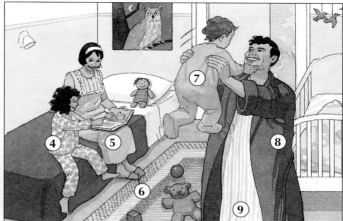

1. leotard/body suit
2. tank top
3. bike shorts

4. pyjamas
5. nightgown
6. slippers

7. sleeper
8. bathrobe
9. nightshirt

10. undershirt
11. long underwear
12. boxer shorts
13. briefs/jockey shorts
14. athletic supporter/jockstrap
15. socks

16. (bikini) panties
17. underpants
18. girdle
19. garter belt
20. bra(ssiere)
21. camisole

22. full slip
23. half slip
24. knee-highs
25. kneesocks
26. stockings
27. pantyhose/nylons

More vocabulary

lingerie: underwear or sleepwear for women
loungewear: clothing (sometimes sleepwear) people wear around the home

Share your answers.

1. What do you wear when you exercise?
2. What kind of clothing do you wear for sleeping?

Shoes and Accessories

1. sales clerk

2. suspenders

3. shoe department

4. silk scarves*

5. hats

12. sole

13. heel

14. shoelace

15. toe

16. pump

17. high heels

18. boots

19. loafers

20. oxfords

21. hiking boots

22. running shoes / runners

23. track shoes / sneakers / running shoes

24. sandals

*Note: one scarf, two scarves

Talk about the shoes you're wearing today.

I'm wearing a pair of <u>white sandals</u>.

Practise asking a salesperson for help.

Could I try on these <u>sandals</u> in size <u>10</u>?

Do you have any <u>silk scarves</u>?

Where are <u>the hats</u>?

6. purses/handbags

7. display case

8. jewellery

9. necklaces

10. ties

11. belts

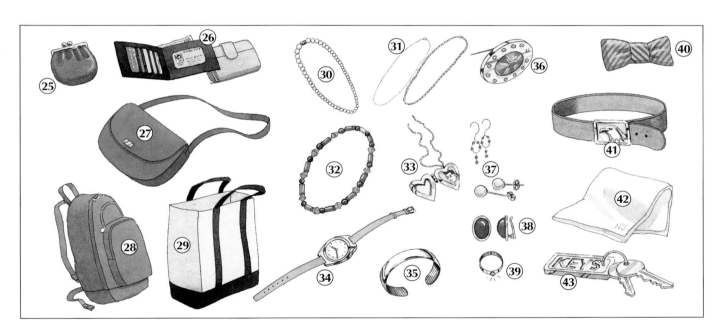

25. change purse

26. wallet

27. shoulder bag

28. backpack/bookbag

29. tote bag

30. string of pearls

31. chain

32. beads

33. locket

34. (wrist)watch

35. bracelet

36. pin/brooch

37. pierced earrings

38. clip-on earrings

39. ring

40. bow tie

41. belt buckle

42. handkerchief

43. key chain

Share your answers.

1. Which of these accessories are usually worn by women? by men?

2. Which of these do you wear every day?

3. Which of these would you wear to a job interview? Why?

4. Which accessory would you like to receive as a present? Why?

Describing Clothes

Sizes

1. extra small   **2.** small   **3.** medium   **4.** large   **5.** extra large

Patterns

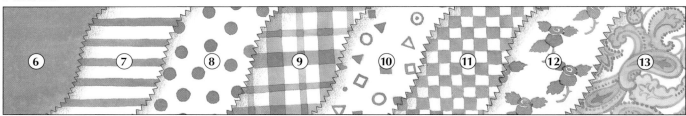

6. solid green   **8.** polka-dotted   **10.** print   **12.** floral

7. striped   **9.** plaid   **11.** checked   **13.** paisley

Types of material

14. wool sweater   **16. cotton** T-shirt   **18. leather** boots

15. silk scarf   **17. linen** jacket   **19. nylon** stockings*

Problems

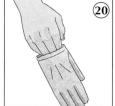    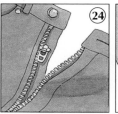 

20. too small   **22.** stain   **24. broken** zipper

21. too big   **23.** rip/tear   **25. missing** button

*Note: Nylon, polyester, rayon, and plastic are synthetic materials.

70

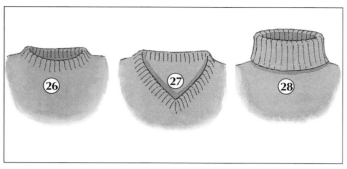

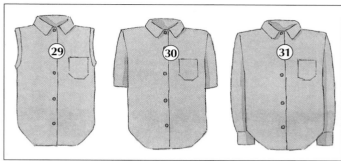

26. crewneck sweater

27. V-neck sweater

28. turtleneck sweater

29. sleeveless shirt

30. short-sleeved shirt

31. long-sleeved shirt

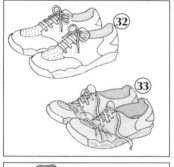

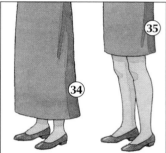

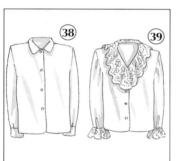

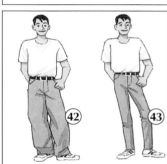

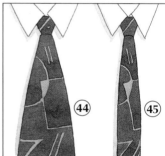

32. new shoes

33. old shoes

34. long skirt

35. short skirt

36. formal dress

37. casual dress

38. plain blouse

39. fancy blouse

40. light jacket

41. heavy jacket

42. loose pants / **baggy** pants

43. tight pants

44. wide tie

45. narrow tie

46. low heels

47. high heels

Talk about yourself.

I like <u>long-sleeved</u> shirts and <u>baggy</u> pants.
I like <u>short skirts</u> and <u>high heels</u>.
I usually wear <u>plain</u> clothes.

Share your answers.

1. What type of material do you usually wear in the summer? in the winter?
2. What patterns do you see around you?
3. Are you wearing casual or formal clothes?

Doing the Laundry

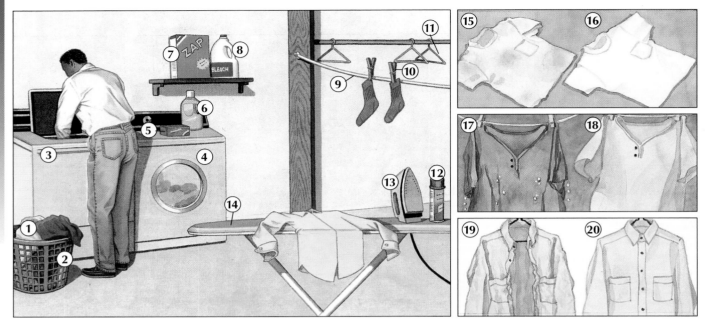

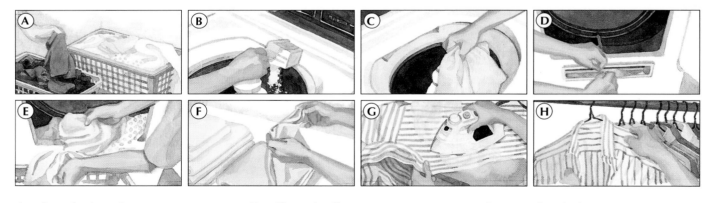

1. laundry	**6.** fabric softener	**11.** hanger	**16. clean** T-shirt
2. laundry basket	**7.** laundry detergent	**12.** spray starch	**17. wet** T-shirt
3. washer	**8.** bleach	**13.** iron	**18. dry** T-shirt
4. dryer	**9.** clothesline	**14.** ironing board	**19. wrinkled** shirt
5. dryer sheets	**10.** clothespin	**15. dirty** T-shirt	**20. ironed / pressed** shirt

A. **Sort** the laundry.

B. **Add** the detergent.

C. **Load** the washer.

D. **Clean** the lint trap.

E. **Unload** the dryer.

F. **Fold** the laundry.

G. **Iron** the clothes.

H. **Hang up** the clothes.

More vocabulary

dry cleaners: a business that cleans clothes using chemicals, not water and detergent

 wash

 dry

 bleach

 iron

 dry clean only

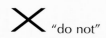 "do not"

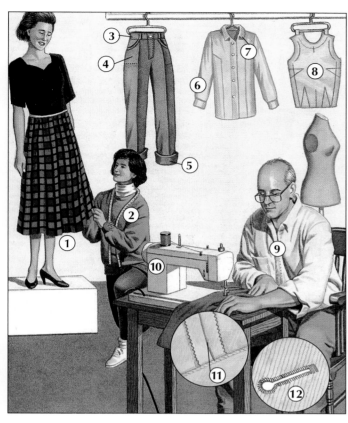

A. **sew** by hand

B. **sew** by machine

C. **lengthen**

D. **shorten**

E. **take in**

F. **let out**

1. hemline

2. dressmaker

3. waistband

4. pocket

5. cuff

6. sleeve

7. collar

8. pattern

9. tailor

10. sewing machine

11. seam

12. buttonhole

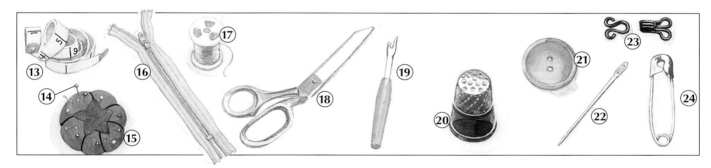

13. tape measure

14. pin

15. pin cushion

16. zipper

17. spool of thread

18. (pair of) scissors

19. seam ripper

20. thimble

21. button

22. needle

23. hook and eye

24. safety pin

More vocabulary

pattern maker: a person who makes patterns

garment worker: a person who works in a clothing factory

fashion designer: a person who makes original clothes

Share your answers.

1. Do you know how to use a sewing machine?

2. Can you sew by hand?

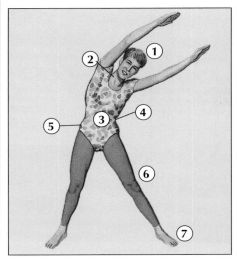

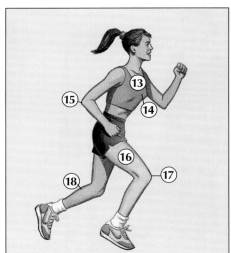

1. head

2. neck

3. abdomen

4. waist

5. hip

6. leg

7. foot

8. hand

9. arm

10. shoulder

11. back

12. buttocks

13. chest

14. breast

15. elbow

16. thigh

17. knee

18. calf

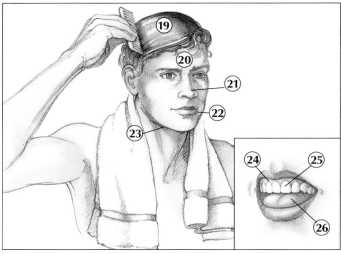

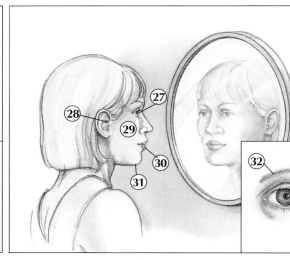

The face

19. hair

20. forehead

21. nose

22. mouth

23. jaw

24. gums

25. teeth

26. tongue

27. eye

28. ear

29. cheek

30. lip

31. chin

32. eyebrow

33. eyelid

34. eyelashes

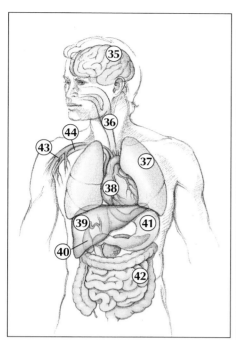

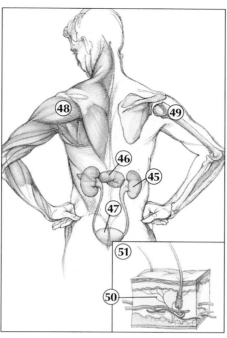

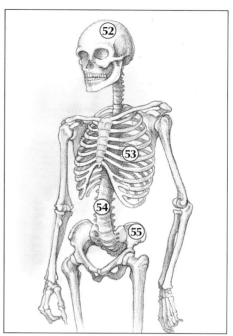

Inside the body

35. brain

36. throat

37. lung

38. heart

39. liver

40. gallbladder

41. stomach

42. intestines

43. artery

44. vein

45. kidney

46. pancreas

47. bladder

48. muscle

49. bone

50. nerve

51. skin

The skeleton

52. skull

53. rib cage

54. spinal column

55. pelvis

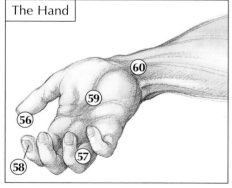

The Hand

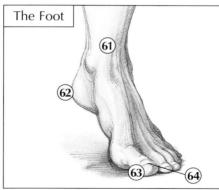

The Foot

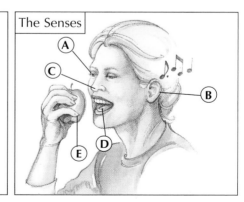

The Senses

56. thumb

57. fingers

58. fingernail

59. palm

60. wrist

61. ankle

62. heel

63. toe

64. toenail

A. see

B. hear

C. smell

D. taste

E. touch

Personal Hygiene

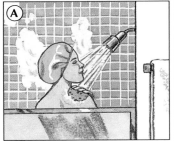

A. take a shower   **B. bathe/take** a bath   **C. use** deodorant   **D. put on** sunscreen

1. shower cap

2. soap

3. bath powder/talcum powder

4. deodorant

5. perfume/cologne

6. sunscreen

7. body lotion

8. moisturizer

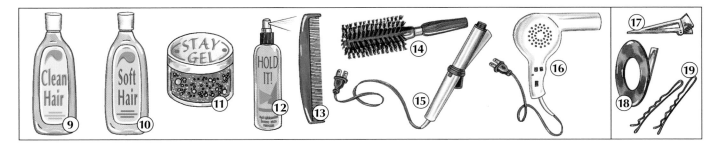

E. wash…hair   **F. rinse**…hair   **G. comb**…hair   **H. dry**…hair   **I. brush**…hair

9. shampoo

10. conditioner

11. hair gel

12. hair spray

13. comb

14. brush

15. curling iron

16. blow dryer

17. hair clip

18. barrette

19. bobby pins

J. brush…teeth

K. floss…teeth

L. gargle

M. shave

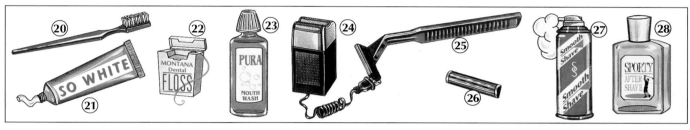

20. toothbrush

21. toothpaste

22. dental floss

23. mouthwash

24. electric shaver

25. razor

26. razor blade

27. shaving cream

28. aftershave

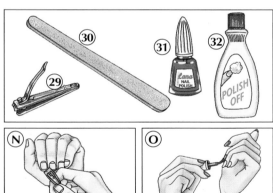

N. cut…nails

O. polish…nails

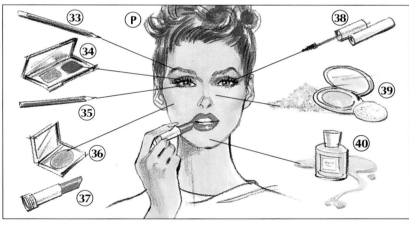
P. put on…makeup

29. nail clipper

30. emery board/nail file

31. nail polish

32. nail polish remover

33. eyebrow pencil

34. eye shadow

35. eyeliner

36. blush/rouge

37. lipstick

38. mascara

39. face powder

40. foundation

More vocabulary

A product without perfume or scent is **unscented.**

A product that is better for people with allergies is **hypoallergenic.**

Share your answers.

1. What is your morning routine if you stay home? if you go out?

2. Do women in your culture wear makeup? How old are they when they begin to use it?

Symptoms and Injuries

1. headache
2. toothache
3. earache
4. stomachache
5. backache

6. sore throat
7. nasal congestion
8. fever/temperature
9. chills
10. rash

A. **cough**
B. **sneeze**
C. **feel** dizzy
D. **feel** nauseous
E. **throw up/vomit**

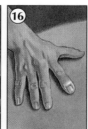

11. insect bite
12. bruise
13. cut

14. sunburn
15. blister
16. **swollen** finger

17. **bloody** nose/nosebleed
18. **sprained** ankle

Use the new language.
Look at **Health Care,** pages **80–81.**
Tell what medication or treatment you would use for each health problem.

Share your answers.
1. For which problems would you go to a doctor? use medication? do nothing?
2. What do you do for a sunburn? for a headache?

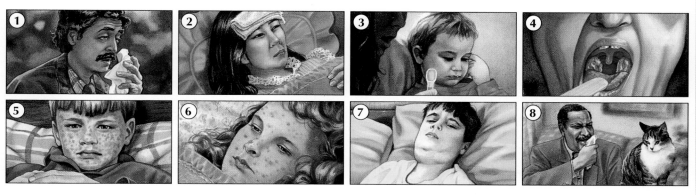

Common illnesses and childhood diseases

1. cold

2. flu

3. ear infection

4. strep throat

5. measles

6. chicken pox

7. mumps

8. allergies

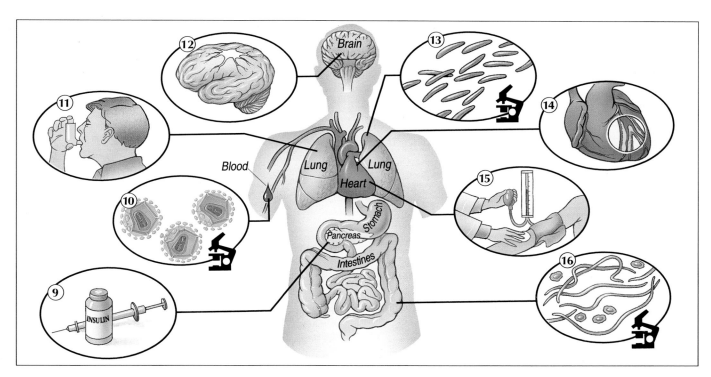

Medical conditions and serious diseases

9. diabetes

10. HIV (human immunodeficiency virus)

11. asthma

12. brain cancer

13. TB (tuberculosis)

14. heart disease

15. high blood pressure

16. intestinal parasites

More vocabulary

AIDS (acquired immunodeficiency syndrome): a medical condition that results from contracting the HIV virus

influenza: flu

hypertension: high blood pressure

infectious disease: a disease that is spread through air or water

Share your answers.

Which diseases on this page are infectious?

Health Care

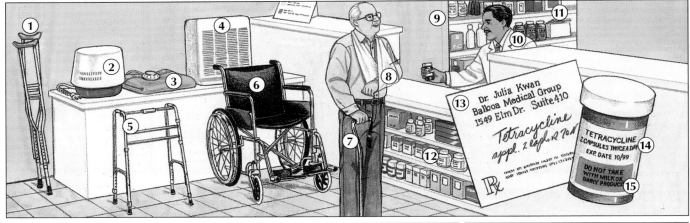

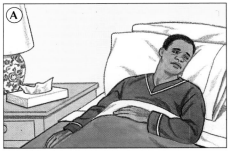  

1. crutches

2. humidifier

3. heating pad

4. air purifier

5. walker

6. wheelchair

7. cane

8. sling

9. pharmacy

10. pharmacist

11. prescription medication

12. over-the-counter medication

13. prescription

14. prescription label

15. warning label

A. **Get** bed rest.

B. **Drink** fluids.

C. **Change** your diet.

D. **Exercise.**

E. **Get** an injection.

F. **Take** medicine.

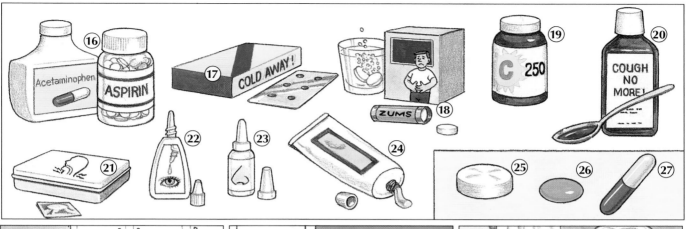

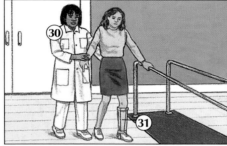

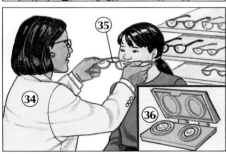
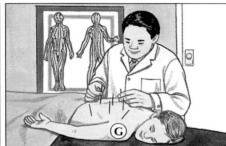
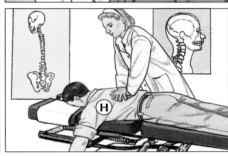

16. pain reliever

17. cold tablets

18. antacid

19. vitamins

20. cough syrup

21. throat lozenges

22. eye drops

23. nasal spray

24. ointment

25. tablet

26. pill

27. capsule

28. orthopedist

29. cast

30. physiotherapist

31. brace

32. audiologist

33. hearing aid

34. optometrist

35. (eye)glasses

36. contact lenses

G. **Get** acupuncture.

H. **Go** to a chiropractor.

Share your answers.

1. What's the best treatment for a headache? a sore throat? a stomachache? a fever?

2. Do you think vitamins are important? Why or why not?

3. What treatments are popular in your culture?

Medical Emergencies

A. **be injured / be hurt**

B. **be** unconscious

C. **be** in shock

D. **have** a heart attack

E. **have** an allergic reaction

F. **get** an electric shock

G. **get** frostbite

H. **burn** (your)self

I. **drown**

J. **swallow** poison

K. **overdose** on drugs

L. **choke**

M. **bleed**

N. **can't breathe**

O. **fall**

P. **break** a bone

Grammar point: past tense

burn	— burned	choke	— choked	bleed	— bled
drown	— drowned	be	— was, were	can't	— couldn't
swallow	— swallowed	have	— had	fall	— fell
overdose	— overdosed	get	— got	break	— broke

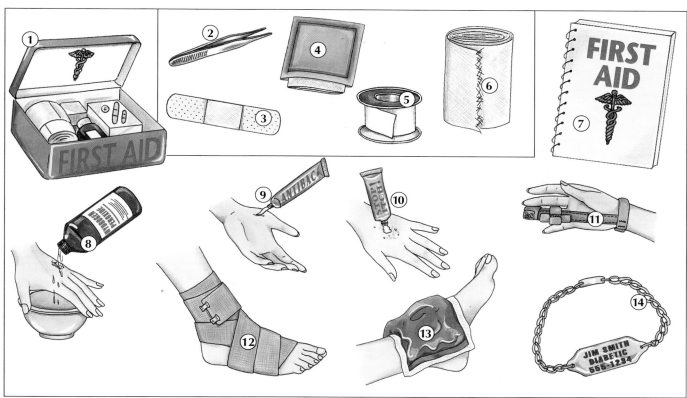

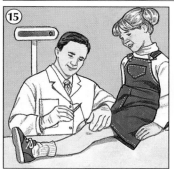 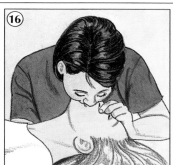 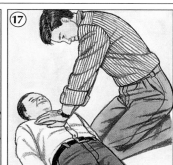 

1. first aid kit

2. tweezers

3. adhesive bandage

4. sterile pad

5. tape

6. gauze

7. first aid manual

8. hydrogen peroxide

9. antibacterial ointment

10. antihistamine cream

11. splint

12. elastic bandage

13. ice pack

14. medical alert bracelet

15. stitches

16. artificial respiration/ mouth-to-mouth

17. CPR (cardiopulmonary resuscitation)

18. Heimlich manoeuvre

Important Note: Only people who are properly trained should give stitches or do CPR.

Share your answers.

1. Do you have a First Aid kit in your home? Where can you buy one?

2. When do you use hydrogen peroxide? an elastic support bandage? antihistamine cream?

3. Do you know first aid? Where did you learn it?

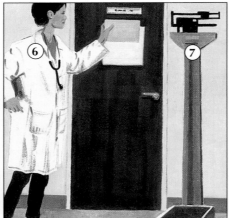

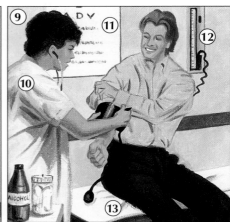

Medical clinic

1. waiting room
2. receptionist
3. patient
4. health card
5. medical information form

6. doctor
7. scale
8. stethoscope
9. examining room
10. nurse

11. eye chart
12. blood pressure gauge
13. examination table
14. syringe
15. thermometer

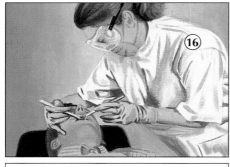

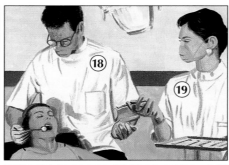

Dental clinic

16. dental hygienist
17. tartar
18. dentist

19. dental assistant
20. cavity
21. drill

22. filling
23. orthodontist
24. braces

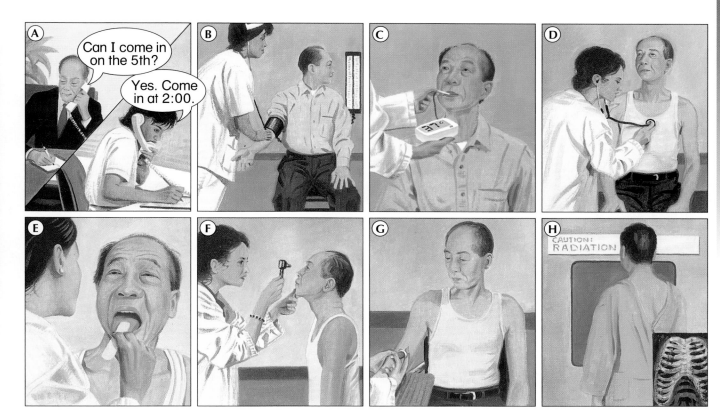

A. **make** an appointment	**D.** **listen** to…heart	**G.** **draw**…blood
B. **check**…blood pressure	**E.** **look** in…throat	**H.** **get** an X-ray
C. **take**…temperature	**F.** **examine**…eyes	

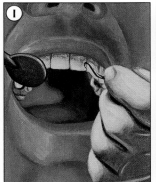
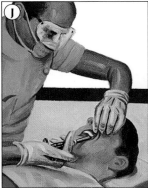

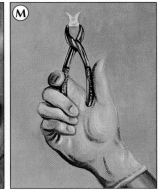

I. **clean**…teeth	**K.** **drill** a tooth	**M.** **pull** a tooth
J. **give**…a shot of anaesthetic/ freezing	**L.** **fill** a cavity	

More vocabulary

get a checkup: to go for a medical exam

extract a tooth: to pull out a tooth

Share your answers.

1. How often should you go for a medical checkup?
2. Some people are nervous at the dentist's office. What can they do to relax?

A Hospital

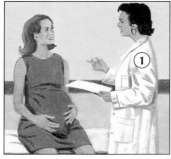
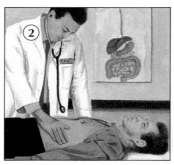

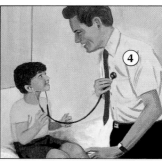
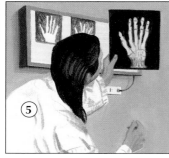

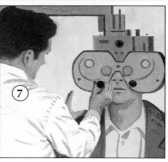
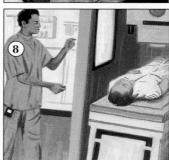

Hospital staff

1. obstetrician
2. internist
3. cardiologist

4. pediatrician
5. radiologist
6. psychiatrist

7. ophthalmologist
8. X-ray technician

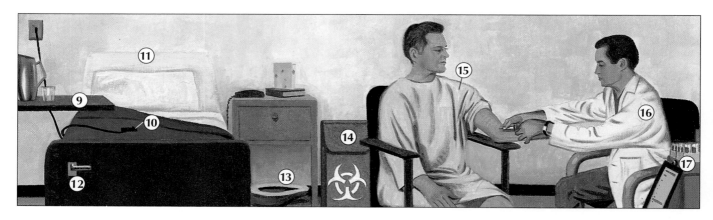

Patient's room

9. bed table
10. call button
11. hospital bed

12. bed control
13. bedpan
14. medical waste disposal

15. hospital gown
16. lab technician
17. blood work/blood test

More vocabulary

nurse practitioner: a nurse licenced to give medical exams

specialist: a doctor who only treats specific medical problems

gynecologist: a specialist who examines and treats women

midwife: someone who is trained to help women in childbirth

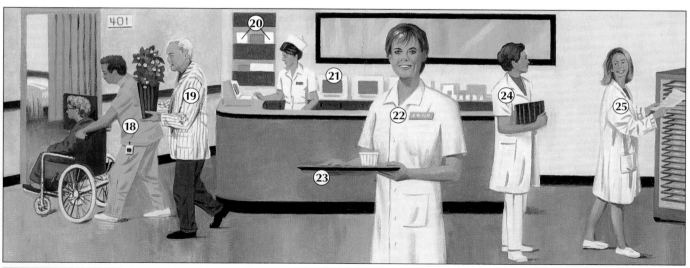

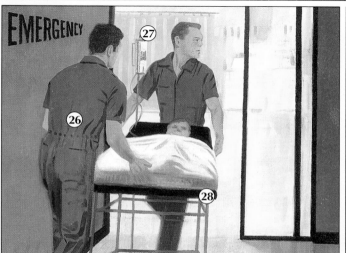

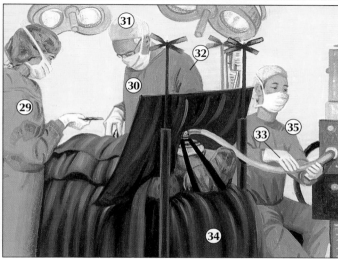

Nurse's station

18. orderly

19. volunteer

20. medical charts

21. vital signs monitor

22. RN (registered nurse)

23. medication tray

24. RNA (registered nursing assistant)

25. dietician

Emergency room

26. paramedic

27. IV (intravenous drip)

28. stretcher/gurney

Operating room

29. surgical nurse

30. surgeon

31. surgical cap

32. surgical gown

33. latex gloves

34. operating table

35. anaesthetist

Practise asking for the hospital staff.

Please get the nurse. I have a question for her.
Where's the anaesthetist? I need to talk to her.
I'm looking for the lab technician. Have you seen him?

Share your answers.

1. Have you ever been to an emergency room? Who helped you?

2. Have you ever been in the hospital? How long did you stay?

City Streets

1. fire station
2. coffee shop
3. bank
4. car dealership
5. hotel

6. church
7. hospital
8. park
9. synagogue
10. theatre

11. movie theatre
12. gas station
13. furniture store
14. hardware store
15. barber shop

More vocabulary

skyscraper: a very tall office building

downtown/city centre: the area in a city with the city hall, courts, and businesses

Practise giving your destination.

I'm going to go <u>downtown</u>.

I have to go to <u>the post office</u>.

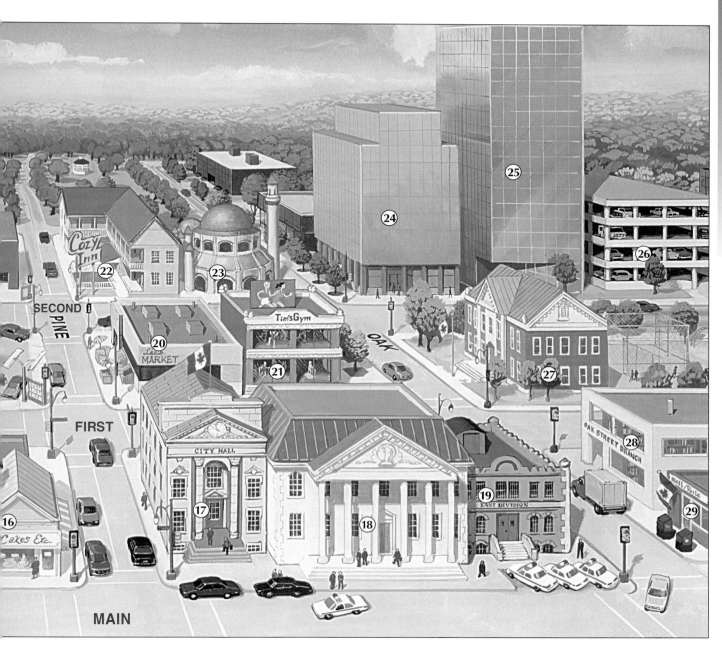

16. bakery

17. city hall

18. courthouse

19. police station

20. grocery store

21. health club

22. motel

23. mosque

24. office building

25. high-rise building

26. parking garage

27. school

28. library

29. post office

Practise asking for and giving the locations of buildings.

Where's the post office?

  It's on Oak Street.

Share your answers.

1. Which of the places in this picture do you go to every week?

2. Is it good to live in a city? Why or why not?

3. What famous cities do you know?

An Intersection

1. Laundromat

2. drugstore/pharmacy

3. convenience store

4. photo shop

5. parking space

6. traffic light

7. pedestrian

8. crosswalk

9. street

10. curb

11. newsstand

12. mailbox

13. drive-thru window

14. fast food restaurant

15. bus

A. **cross** the street

B. **wait** for the light

C. **drive** a car

More vocabulary

neighbourhood: the area close to your home

do errands: to make a short trip from your home to buy or pick up something

Talk about where to buy things.

You can buy newspapers at a newsstand.

You can buy donuts at a donut shop.

You can buy food at a convenience store.

16. bus stop	**22.** copy centre/print shop	**28.** fire hydrant
17. corner	**23.** streetlight	**29.** sign
18. parking meter	**24.** dry cleaners	**30.** street vendor
19. motorcycle	**25.** nail salon	**31.** cart
20. donut shop	**26.** sidewalk	**D. park** the car
21. public telephone/pay phone	**27.** garbage truck	**E. ride** a bicycle

Share your answers.

1. Do you like to do errands?

2. Do you always like to go to the same stores?

3. Which businesses in the picture are also in your neighbourhood?

4. Do you know someone who has a small business? What kind?

5. What things can you buy from a street vendor?

A Mall

1. music store

2. jewellery store

3. candy store

4. bookstore

5. toy store

6. pet store

7. card store

8. optician

9. travel agency

10. shoe store

11. fountain

12. florist

More vocabulary

beauty shop: hair salon

men's store: a store that sells men's clothing

dress shop: a store that sells women's clothing

Talk about where you want to shop in this mall.

Let's go to the card store.

I need to buy a card for Maggie's birthday.

13. department store

14. food court

15. video store

16. hair salon

17. maternity shop

18. electronics store

19. directory

20. ice cream stand

21. escalator

22. information booth

Practise asking for and giving the location of different shops.

Where's <u>the maternity shop?</u>

   It's on <u>the first floor</u>, next to <u>the hair salon.</u>

Share your answers.

1. Do you like shopping malls? Why or why not?

2. Some people don't go to the mall to shop.
Name some other things you can do in a mall.

A Childcare Centre

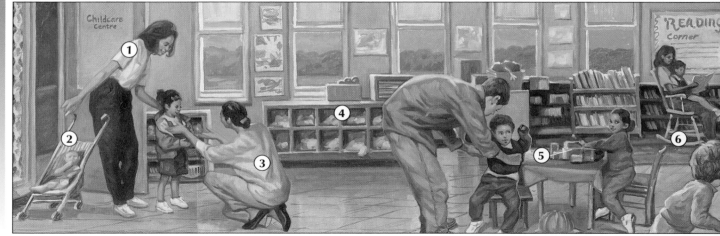

1. parent

2. stroller

3. childcare worker

4. cubby

5. toys

6. rocking chair

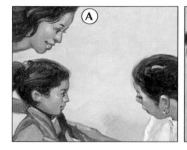

A. **drop off**

B. **hold**

C. **nurse**

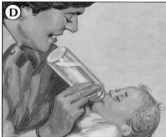

D. **feed**

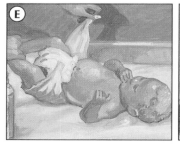

E. **change** diapers

F. **read** a story

G. **pick up**

H. **rock**

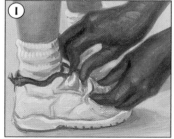

I. **tie** shoes

J. **dress**

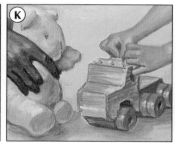

K. **play**

L. **take** a nap

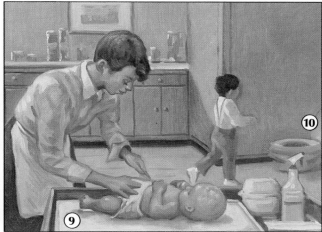

7. high chair   **8.** bib   **9.** change table   **10.** potty seat

11. playpen

12. walker

13. car (safety) seat

14. baby carrier

15. baby backpack

16. carriage

17. wipes

18. baby powder

19. disinfectant

20. disposable diapers

21. cloth diapers

22. diaper pins

23. diaper pail

24. training pants

25. formula

26. bottle

27. nipple

28. baby food

29. pacifier/soother

30. teething ring

31. rattle

Canada Post

1. envelope

2. letter

3. postcard

4. greeting card

5. package/parcel

6. letter carrier

7. return address

8. mailing address

9. postmark

10. stamp/postage

11. registered mail

12. priority courier

13. airmail envelope

14. surface mail/parcel post

15. Express Post

Emily Kitowski
1543 Oak Lane
Montréal, QC
H9B 3G5 ⑦

MONTRÉAL
5-7-99
QC ⑨

⑩

Alyson Shepard
249 Courtney Drive
Sudbury, ON
P3E 2B9 ⑧

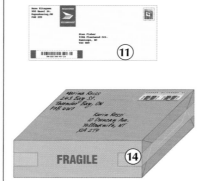

A. **address** a postcard

B. **send** it/**mail** it

C. **deliver** it

D. **receive** it

1. teller

2. vault

3. bank machine / automated teller machine

4. security guard

5. passbook

6. savings account number

7. cheque book

8. chequing account number

9. bank card

10. monthly statement

11. balance

12. deposit slip

13. safety deposit box

Using the bank machine

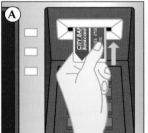

A. **Insert** your bank card.

B. **Enter** your PIN number.*

C. **Make** a deposit.

D. **Withdraw** cash.

E. **Transfer** funds.

F. **Remove** your bank card.

*PIN: personal identification number

More vocabulary

overdrawn account: When there is not enough money in an account to pay a cheque, we say the account is overdrawn.

Share your answers.

1. Do you use a bank?

2. Do you use a bank card?

3. Name some things you can put in a safety deposit box.

1. reference librarian	**7.** magazine	**13.** videocassette	**19.** library card
2. reference desk	**8.** newspaper	**14.** CD (compact disc)	**20.** library book
3. atlas	**9.** online catalogue	**15.** record	**21.** title
4. microfilm reader	**10.** card catalogue	**16.** checkout desk	**22.** author
5. microfilm	**11.** media section	**17.** library clerk	
6. periodical section	**12.** audiocassette	**18.** encyclopedia	

More vocabulary

check a book out: to borrow a book from the library

non-fiction: real information, history or true stories

fiction: stories from the author's imagination

Share your answers.

1. Do you have a library card?
2. Do you prefer to buy books or borrow them from the library?

A. arrest a suspect

1. police officer

2. handcuffs

B. hire a lawyer

3. guard

4. defence lawyer/defence counsel

C. appear in court

5. defendant

6. judge

D. stand trial

7. courtroom

8. jury

9. evidence

10. Crown counsel

11. witness

12. court reporter

13. bailiff

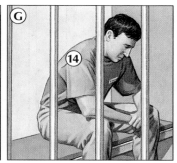

E. give the verdict*

F. sentence the defendant

G. go to jail/**go** to prison

14. convict

H. be released

*Note: There are two possible verdicts, "guilty" and "not guilty."

Share your answers.

1. What are some differences between the legal system in Canada and the one in your country?

2. Do you want to be on a jury? Why or why not?

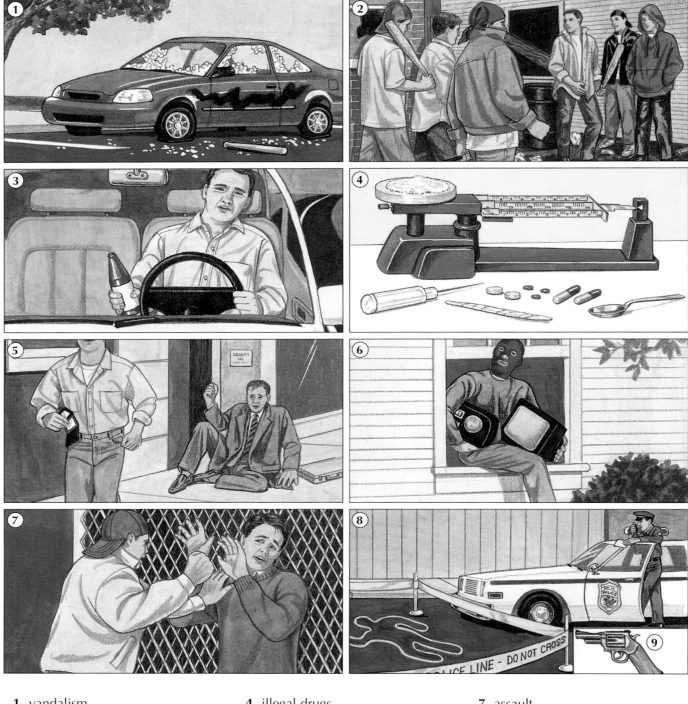

1. vandalism

2. gang violence

3. drunk driving/impaired driving

4. illegal drugs

5. mugging

6. burglary

7. assault

8. murder

9. gun

More vocabulary

commit a crime: to do something illegal

criminal: someone who commits a crime

victim: someone who is hurt or killed by someone else

Share your answers.

1. Is there too much crime on TV? in the movies?

2. Do you think people become criminals from watching crime on TV?

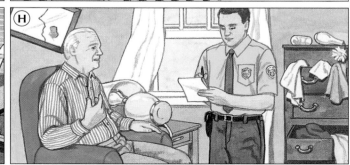

A. **Walk** with a friend.

B. **Stay** on well-lit streets.

C. **Hold** your purse close to your body.

D. **Protect** your wallet.

E. **Lock** your doors.

F. **Don't open** your door to strangers.

G. **Don't drink** and **drive**.

H. **Report** crimes to the police.

More vocabulary

Neighbourhood Watch: a group of neighbours who watch for criminals in their neighbourhood

designated drivers: people who don't drink alcoholic beverages so that they can drive drinkers home

Share your answers.

1. Do you feel safe in your neighbourhood?
2. Look at the pictures. Which of these things do you do?
3. What other things do you do to stay safe?

Emergencies and Natural Disasters

1. lost child

2. car accident

3. airplane crash

4. explosion

5. earthquake

6. mudslide

7. fire

8. firefighter

9. fire truck

Practise reporting a fire.

This is Lisa Broad. There is a fire.

The address is 323 Oak Street.

Please send someone quickly.

Share your answers.

1. Can you give directions to your home if there is a fire?

2. What information do you give to the other driver if you are in a car accident?

10. drought

11. blizzard

12. hurricane

13. tornado

14. volcanic eruption

15. tidal wave

16. flood

17. search and rescue team

Share your answers.

1. Which disasters are common in your area? Which never happen?

2. What can you do to prepare for emergencies?

3. Do you have emergency numbers near your telephone?

4. What organizations will help you in an emergency?

103

Public Transportation

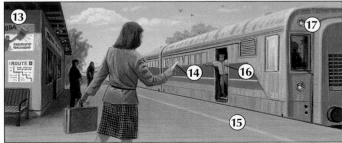

1. bus stop	**7.** passenger	**13.** train station	**19.** taxi stand
2. route	**8.** bus driver	**14.** ticket	**20.** taxi driver
3. schedule	**9.** subway	**15.** platform	**21.** meter
4. bus	**10.** track	**16.** conductor	**22.** taxi licence
5. fare	**11.** token	**17.** train	**23.** ferry
6. transfer	**12.** transit pass	**18.** taxi / cab	

More vocabulary

hail a taxi: to get a taxi driver's attention by raising your hand

miss the bus: to arrive at the bus stop late

Talk about how you and your friends come to school.

I take <u>the bus</u> to school.   *He <u>drives</u> to school.*
You take <u>the train</u>.   *She <u>walks</u> to school.*
We take <u>the subway</u>.   *They <u>ride</u> bikes.*

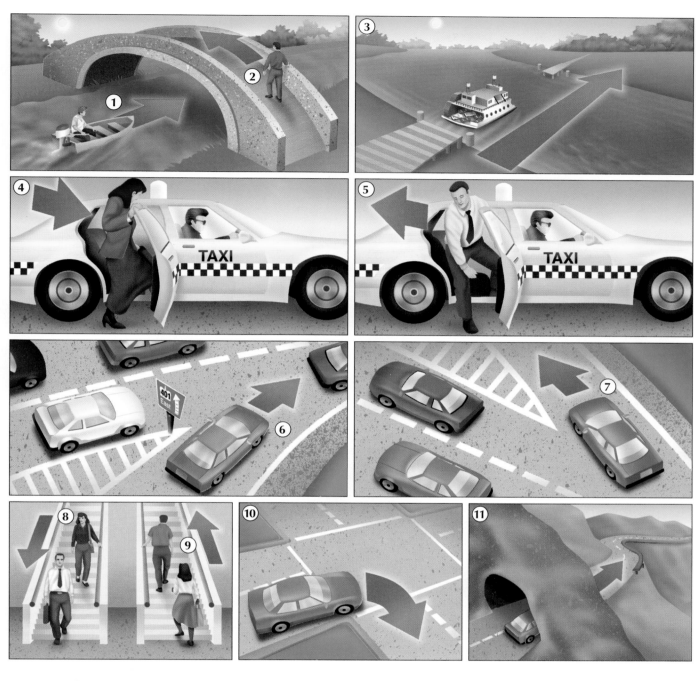

1. **under** the bridge

2. **over** the bridge

3. **across** the water

4. **into** the taxi

5. **out of** the taxi

6. **onto** the highway

7. **off** the highway

8. **down** the stairs

9. **up** the stairs

10. **around** the corner

11. **through** the tunnel

Grammar point: *into, out of, on, off*

We say, *get **into** a taxi or a car.*
But we say, *get **on** a bus, a train, or a plane.*

We say, *get **out of** a taxi or a car.*
But we say, *get **off** a bus, a train, or a plane.*

Cars and Trucks

1. subcompact

2. compact

3. midsize car

4. full-size car

5. convertible

6. sports car

7. pickup truck

8. station wagon

9. sport utility vehicle

10. minivan

11. RV (recreational vehicle)

12. dump truck

13. tow truck

14. moving van

15. tractor trailer/semi

16. cab

17. trailer

More vocabulary

make: the name of the company that makes the car

model: the style of car

Share your answers.

1. What is your favourite kind of car?

2. What kind of car is good for a big family? for a single person?

Directions

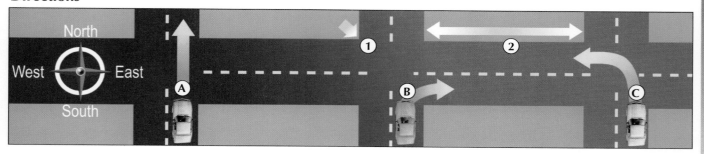

A. go straight

B. turn right

C. turn left

1. corner

2. block

Signs

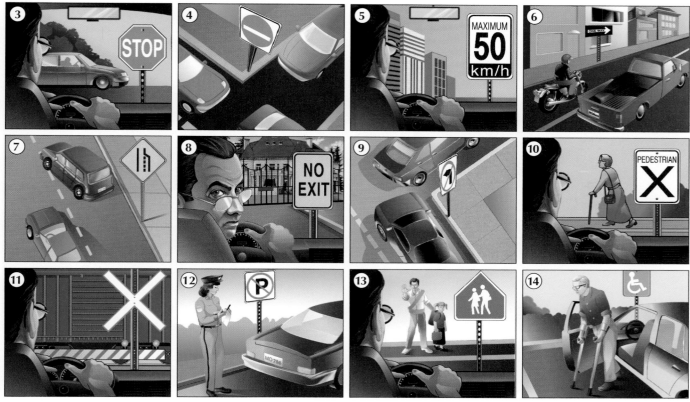

3. stop

4. do not enter/wrong way

5. speed limit

6. one way

7. right lane ends

8. no exit

9. no left turn

10. pedestrian crossing

11. railroad crossing

12. no parking

13. school crossing

14. handicapped parking

More vocabulary

right-of-way: the right to go first

yield: to give another person or car the right-of-way

Share your answers.

1. Which traffic signs are the same in your country?

2. Do pedestrians have the right-of-way in your city?

3. What is the speed limit in front of your school? your home?

Parts of a Car and Car Maintenance

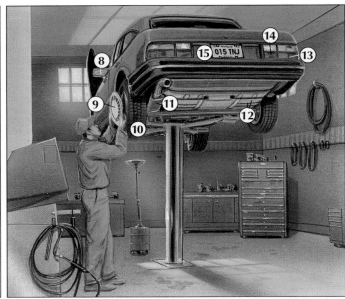

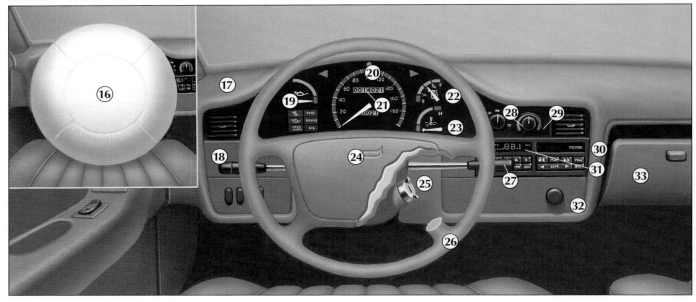

1. rearview mirror	**10.** tire	**19.** oil gauge	**28.** air conditioning
2. windshield	**11.** muffler	**20.** speedometer	**29.** heater
3. windshield wipers	**12.** gas tank	**21.** odometer	**30.** tape deck
4. turn signal	**13.** brake light	**22.** gas gauge	**31.** radio
5. headlight	**14.** tail light	**23.** temperature gauge	**32.** cigarette lighter
6. hood	**15.** licence plate	**24.** horn	**33.** glove compartment
7. bumper	**16.** air bag	**25.** ignition	
8. sideview mirror	**17.** dashboard	**26.** steering wheel	
9. hubcap	**18.** turn signal	**27.** gearshift	

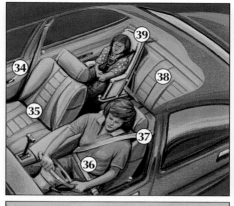
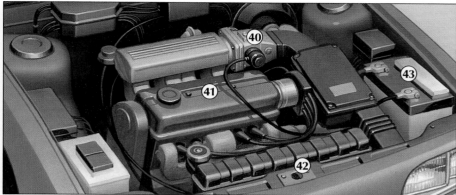
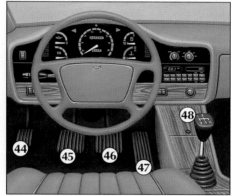

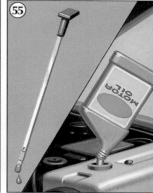

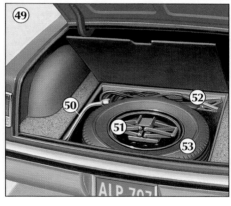

34. lock

35. front seat

36. seat belt

37. shoulder strap

38. back seat

39. child safety seat/car seat

40. fuel injection system

41. engine

42. radiator

43. battery

44. emergency brake

45. clutch*

46. brake pedal

47. accelerator/gas pedal

48. stick shift

49. trunk

50. lug wrench

51. jack

52. jumper cables

53. spare tire

54. The car needs **gas**.

55. The car needs **oil**.

56. The radiator needs **coolant**.

57. The car needs **a pollution control check.**

58. The battery needs **recharging**.

59. The tires need **air**.

*Note: Standard transmission cars have a clutch; automatic transmission cars do not.

109

1. airline terminal	**9.** airplane	**17.** baggage claim area
2. airline representative	**10.** overhead compartment	**18.** carousel
3. check-in counter	**11.** cockpit	**19.** luggage carrier
4. arrival and departure monitors	**12.** pilot	**20.** customs
5. gate	**13.** flight attendant	**21.** customs officer
6. boarding area	**14.** oxygen mask	**22.** declaration form
7. control tower	**15.** airsickness bag	**23.** passenger
8. helicopter	**16.** tray table	

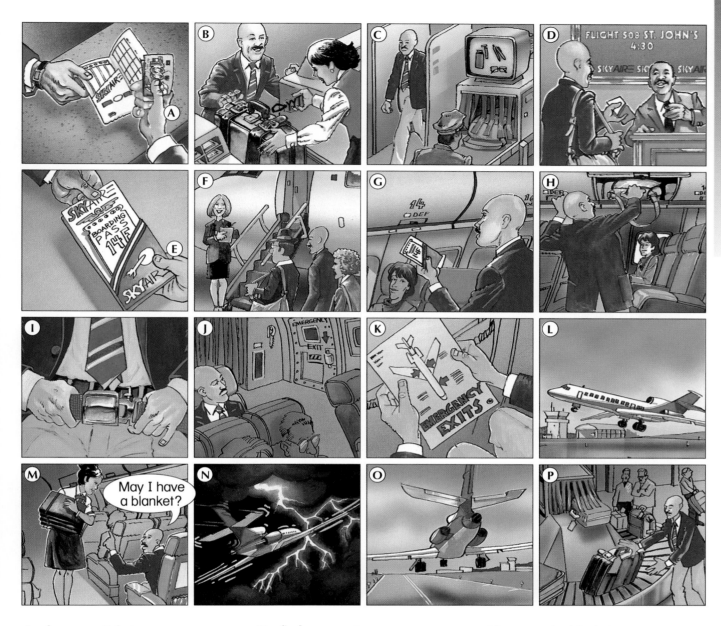

A. **buy** your ticket

B. **check** your bags

C. **go through** security

D. **check in** at the gate

E. **get** your boarding pass

F. **board** the plane

G. **find** your seat

H. **stow** your carry-on bag

I. **fasten** your seat belt

J. **look for** the emergency exit

K. **look at** the emergency card

L. **take off / leave**

M. **request** a blanket

N. **experience** turbulence

O. **land / arrive**

P. **claim** your baggage

More vocabulary

destination: the place the passenger is going
departure time: the time the plane takes off
arrival time: the time the plane lands

direct flight: a plane trip between two cities with no stops
stopover: a stop before reaching the destination, sometimes to change planes

1. public school

2. private school

3. separate school/Catholic school/
denominational school

4. preschool

5. elementary school

6. middle school/
junior high school

7. high school

8. adult school

9. vocational school/trade school

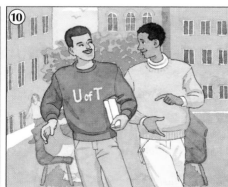

10. college/university

Note: In Canada most children begin school at age 4 or 5
(in kindergarten) and graduate from high school at 17 or 18.

More vocabulary

When students graduate from a college or university
they receive a **degree**:

Bachelor's degree — usually 4 years of study

Master's degree — an additional 1–3 years of study

Doctorate — an additional 3–5 years of study

community college: a school that offers
training/instruction in particular occupations or
professions and gives degrees or diplomas

graduate school: a school in a university where students
study for their master's and doctorates

1. writing assignment

A. Write a first draft.

B. Edit your paper.

C. Get feedback.

D. Rewrite your paper.

E. Turn in your paper.

2. paper / composition

③

④ **My life in Canada**

⑤ I arrived in this country in 1996. My family did not come with me. I was homesick, nervous, and a little excited. I had no job and no friends here. I lived with my aunt and my daily routine was always the same: get up, look for a job, go to bed. At night I remembered my mother's words to me, "Son, you can always come home!" I was homesick and scared, but I did not go home.

I started to study English at night. English is a difficult language and many times I was too tired to study. One teacher, Mrs. Armstrong, was very kind to me. She showed me many

3. title

4. sentence

5. paragraph

Punctuation

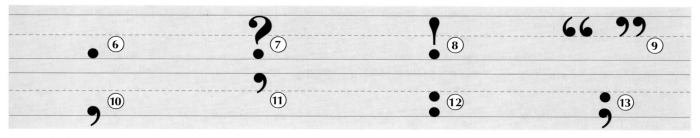

6. period

7. question mark

8. exclamation mark

9. quotation marks

10. comma

11. apostrophe

12. colon

13. semicolon

Government and Citizenship in Canada

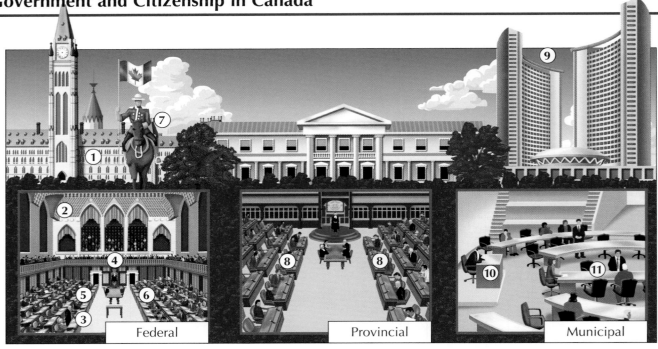

Federal

Provincial

Municipal

1. Parliament building

2. House of Commons

3. Prime Minister

4. Speaker of the House

5. Members of Parliament (MPs)

6. Opposition

7. Mountie

8. members of provincial legislature

9. city hall

10. mayor

11. city councillors

Citizenship application requirements

A. **be** 18 years old

B. **live** in Canada for three years

C. **speak** some English or French

D. **take** a citizenship test

Rights and responsibilities

E. **vote**

F. **obey** the law

G. **respect** the rights of others

H. **care** for Canada's heritage

Aboriginal peoples live throughout what is now Canada

986
Vikings reach east coast of North America

1497
John Cabot claims Newfoundland for Britain

1534–1541
Jacques Cartier makes three voyages to the New World and claims land for France

1605
Samuel de Champlain establishes first settlement at Port Royal in present-day Nova Scotia

1663
Royal colony of New France is established; the fur trade and fishing are the main industries

1670
Hudson's Bay Company is founded and is granted a large area of land in the interior of the continent; fur trade expands

Beaver pelts were in great demand for the fur trade.

1759
British defeat French at Battle of the Plains of Abraham; French rule ends

1812
War of 1812; Canada fights with Britain against Americans and British North America remains British

1866
Colony of British Columbia is established

1867
CONFEDERATION
Dominion of Canada is established with four provinces: Ontario, Québec, Nova Scotia, New Brunswick

Canada's Coat of Arms

1869
Red River Rebellion (1st Riel Rebellion)

Canada buys Rupert's Land from Hudson's Bay Co. and gets North-Western Territory from Britain

1870
Province of Manitoba is founded

1871
British Columbia joins Confederation

1873
Prince Edward Island joins Confederation

1885
Canadian Pacific Railway completed

North-West Rebellion (2nd Riel Rebellion) crushed

1898
Yukon becomes a separate territory

1905
Provinces of Alberta and Saskatchewan formed

1914–1918
Canada participates in World War I

1917
Halifax explosion

1918
Women win right to vote in federal elections

1929–1934
Great Depression; many people suffer from unemployment and poverty

1931
Statute of Westminster extends Canada's independence from Britain

1939–1945
Canada participates in World War II

1942
Internment of Japanese Canadians

1949
Newfoundland and Labrador join Canada as the 10th province

1956
Canadian peacekeeping mission in Suez, Egypt; Prime Minister Lester Pearson wins Nobel Peace Prize the following year

1965
Canada gets its new flag with the red maple leaf

1967
Canada celebrates its Centennial; the country is 100 years old

1969
Official Languages Act makes English and French Canada's official languages

1970
October (FLQ) Crisis in Québec

1982
Constitution Act and Charter of Rights and Freedoms signed

1989
Free Trade Agreement with the United States

1994
North American Free Trade Agreement (NAFTA)

1995
People of Québec vote to remain part of Canada by a narrow margin

1999
New territory of Nunavut established in Canada's north

Provincial Symbols

Flags	Flowers	Flags	Flowers
Alberta 	(1)	Nova Scotia 	(7)
British Columbia 	(2)	Nunavut 	(8)
Manitoba 	(3)	Ontario 	(9)
New Brunswick 	(4)	Prince Edward Island 	(10)
Newfoundland	 (5)	Québec 	(11)
Northwest Territories	 (6)	Saskatchewan 	(12)
		Yukon Territory 	(13)

1. wild rose
2. pacific dogwood
3. prairie crocus
4. purple violet

5. pitcher plant
6. mountain avens
7. mayflower
8. purple saxifrage

9. white trillium
10. lady's slipper
11. white garden lily

12. western red lily
13. fireweed

1. rain forest

2. waterfall

3. river

4. desert

5. sand dune

6. ocean

7. peninsula

8. island

9. bay

10. beach

11. forest

12. shore

13. lake

14. mountain peak

15. mountain range

16. hills

17. canyon

18. valley

19. plains/prairies

20. meadow

21. pond

More vocabulary

a body of water: a river, lake, or ocean

stream/creek: a very small river

Talk about where you live and where you like to go.

I live in a valley. There is a lake nearby.

I like to go to the beach.

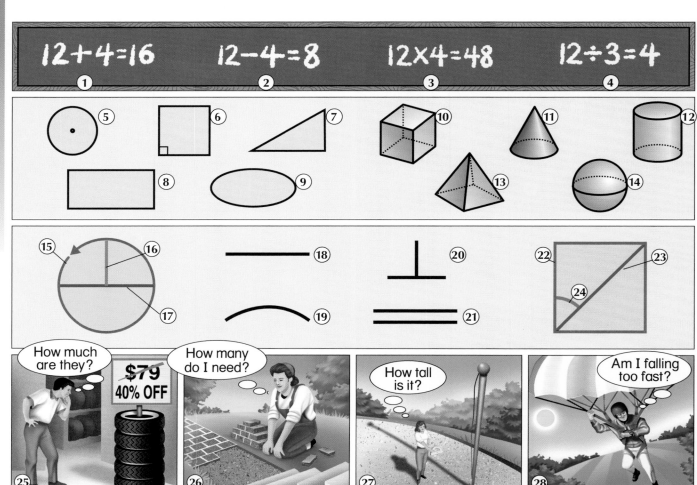

Operations

1. addition
2. subtraction
3. multiplication
4. division

Shapes

5. circle
6. square
7. triangle
8. rectangle
9. oval/ellipse

Solids

10. cube
11. cone
12. cylinder
13. pyramid
14. sphere

Parts of a circle

15. circumference
16. radius
17. diameter

Lines

18. straight
19. curved
20. perpendicular
21. parallel

Parts of a square

22. side
23. diagonal
24. angle

Types of math

25. algebra
26. geometry
27. trigonometry
28. calculus

More vocabulary

total: the answer to an addition problem
difference: the answer to a subtraction problem
product: the answer to a multiplication problem

quotient: the answer to a division problem
pi (π): the number when you divide the circumference of a circle by its diameter (approximately = 3.14)

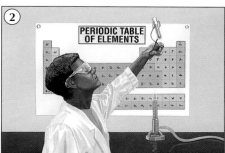

PERIODIC TABLE OF ELEMENTS

$H_2O = water$

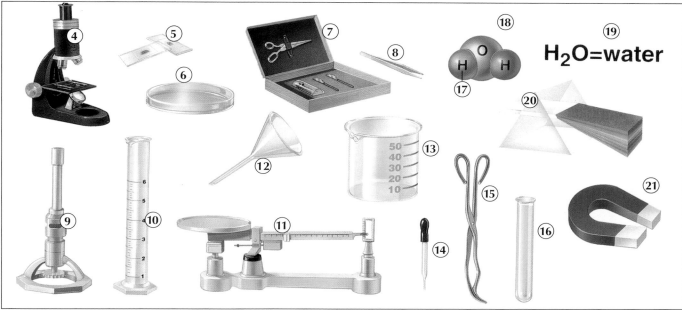

1. biology

2. chemistry

3. physics

4. microscope

5. slide

6. Petri dish

7. dissection kit

8. forceps

9. Bunsen burner

10. graduated cylinder

11. balance

12. funnel

13. beaker

14. dropper

15. crucible tongs

16. test tube

17. atom

18. molecule

19. formula

20. prism

21. magnet

A. **do** an experiment

B. **observe**

C. **record** results

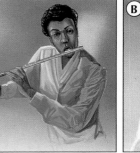

A. **play** an instrument

B. **sing** a song

1. orchestra

2. rock band

Woodwinds

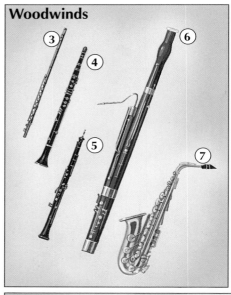

Strings

Brass

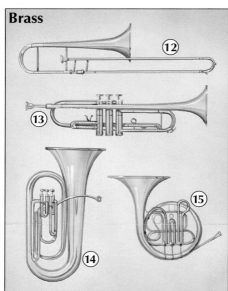

Percussion

Other Instruments

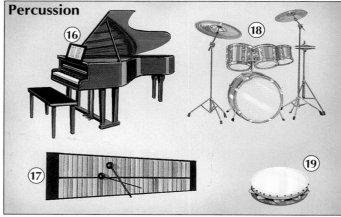

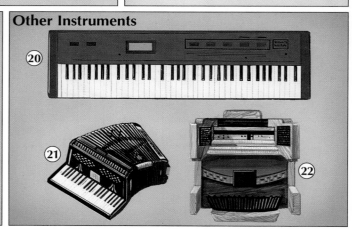

3. flute	**8.** violin	**13.** trumpet/horn	**18.** drums
4. clarinet	**9.** cello	**14.** tuba	**19.** tambourine
5. oboe	**10.** bass	**15.** French horn	**20.** electric keyboard
6. bassoon	**11.** guitar	**16.** piano	**21.** accordion
7. saxophone	**12.** trombone	**17.** xylophone	**22.** organ

It's a chair.

Das ist ein Stuhl.

OUR LEGAL SYSTEM

SUPREME COURT OF CANADA

FEDERAL COURT OF CANADA

PROVINCIAL COURTS

1. art

2. business education

3. choir

4. computer science

5. family studies

6. economics

7. English as a second language

8. foreign language

9. law

10. industrial arts/shop

11. Phys. ed. (physical education)

12. theatre arts/drama

More vocabulary

core course: a subject students have to take

elective: a subject students choose to take

Share your answers.

1. What are your favourite subjects?

2. In your opinion, what subjects are most important? Why?

3. What foreign languages are taught in your school?

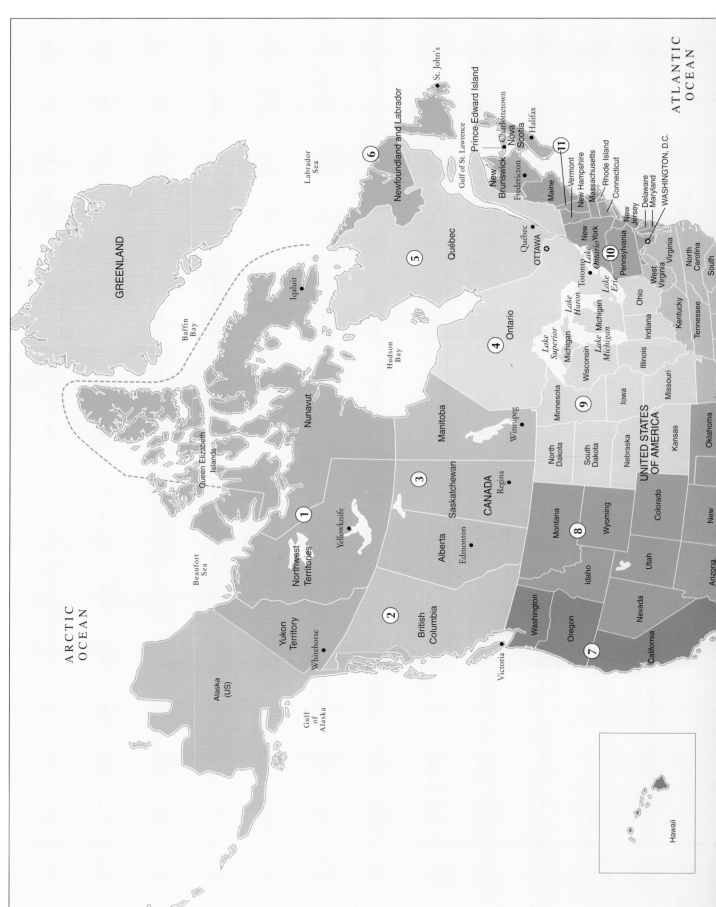

ARCTIC OCEAN

ATLANTIC OCEAN

Beaufort Sea

GREENLAND

Labrador Sea

Baffin Bay

Gulf of Alaska

Alaska (US)

Yukon Territory

Whitehorse

Northwest Territories

Yellowknife

Queen Elizabeth Islands

Nunavut

Iqaluit

Hudson Bay

Newfoundland and Labrador

St. John's

Prince Edward Island

Charlottetown

Gulf of St. Lawrence

Nova Scotia

Halifax

New Brunswick

Fredericton

Maine

Québec

Québec

OTTAWA

Ontario

Vermont

New Hampshire

Massachusetts

Rhode Island

Connecticut

New York

New Jersey

Delaware

Maryland

WASHINGTON, D.C.

Virginia

West Virginia

Toronto

Lake Ontario

Lake Erie

Pennsylvania

Lake Huron

Lake Superior

Lake Michigan

Lake Michigan

Michigan

Wisconsin

Minnesota

Ohio

Indiana

Illinois

Missouri

Iowa

Kentucky

Tennessee

North Carolina

South

Virginia

British Columbia

Victoria

Alberta

Edmonton

Saskatchewan

Regina

Manitoba

Winnipeg

CANADA

Washington

Oregon

Idaho

Montana

Wyoming

Nevada

Utah

Colorado

California

Arizona

New

North Dakota

South Dakota

Nebraska

Kansas

Oklahoma

UNITED STATES OF AMERICA

Hawaii

1 2 3 4 5 6 7 8 9 10 11

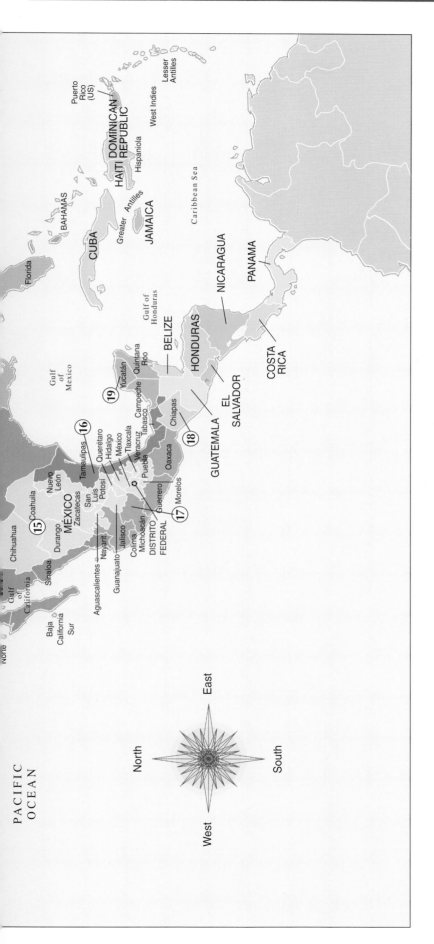

PACIFIC OCEAN

Baja California Sur

Norte

Gulf of California

Chihuahua

Sinaloa

Durango

Coahuila

⑮ MÉXICO

Zacatecas

Nuevo León

San Luis Potosí

Nayarit

Aguascalientes

Jalisco

Guanajuato

Colima

Michoacán

DISTRITO FEDERAL

Querétaro

Hidalgo

México

Tlaxcala

Puebla

Veracruz

Morelos

⑰

Guerrero

Oaxaca

⑯

Tamaulipas

Gulf of Mexico

⑲ Yucatán

Campeche

Tabasco

Quintana Roo

Chiapas

⑱

GUATEMALA

EL SALVADOR

BELIZE

HONDURAS

Gulf of Honduras

NICARAGUA

COSTA RICA

PANAMA

Caribbean Sea

CUBA

BAHAMAS

Florida

JAMAICA

Greater Antilles

HAITI DOMINICAN REPUBLIC

Hispaniola

Puerto Rico (US)

West Indies

Lesser Antilles

East

North

South

West

Regions of Canada

1. Northern Canada

2. British Columbia

3. The Prairie Provinces

4. Ontario

5. Québec

6. The Atlantic Provinces*

*Note: New Brunswick, Nova Scotia, and Prince Edward Island are often referred to as the Maritimes or the Maritime Provinces.

Regions of the United States

7. The Pacific States/the West Coast

8. The Rocky Mountain States

9. The Midwest

10. The Mid-Atlantic States

11. New England

12. The Southwest

13. The Southeast/the South

Regions of Mexico

14. The Pacific Northwest

15. The Plateau of Mexico

16. The Gulf Coastal Plain

17. The Southern Uplands

18. The Chiapas Highlands

19. The Yucatan Peninsula

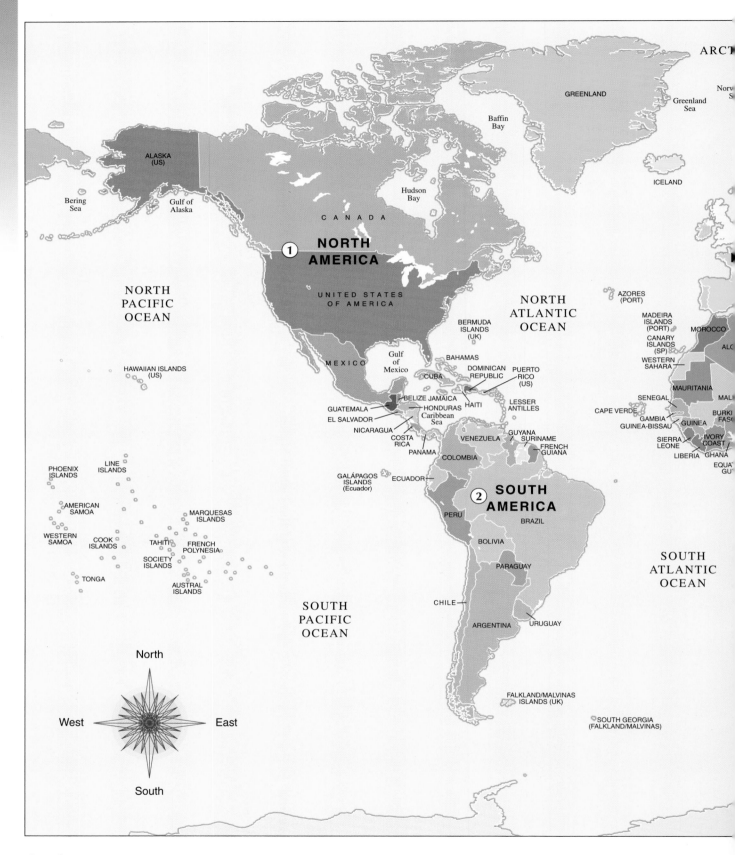

Continents

1. North America

2. South America

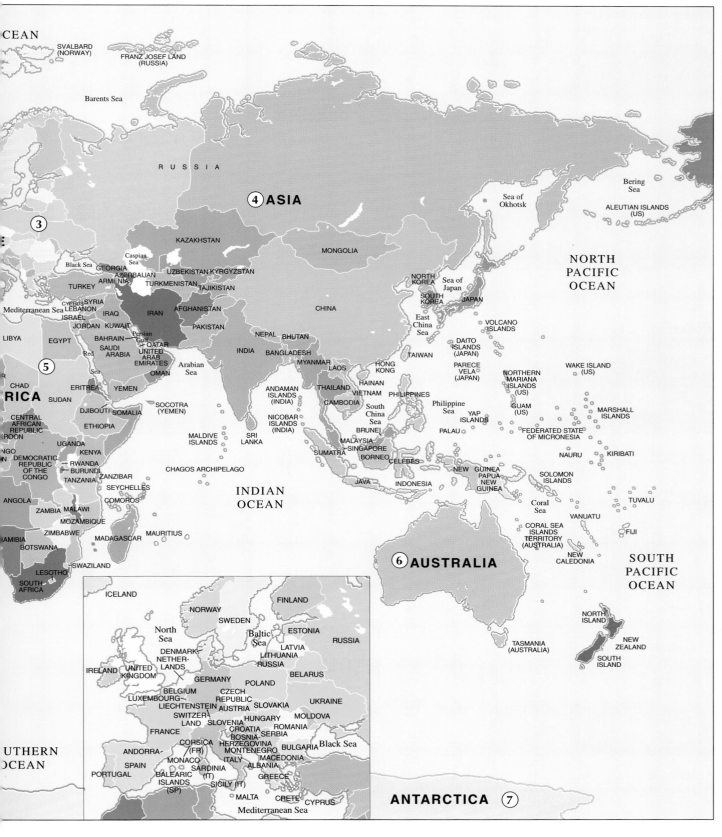

CEAN

SVALBARD
(NORWAY)

FRANZ JOSEF LAND
(RUSSIA)

Barents Sea

R U S S I A

③④ ASIA

③

KAZAKHSTAN

MONGOLIA

Caspian
Sea

Black Sea
GEORGIA
AZERBAIJAN
ARMENIA
TURKEY

UZBEKISTAN KYRGYZSTAN
TURKMENISTAN
TAJIKISTAN

Bering
Sea

ALEUTIAN ISLANDS
(US)

Sea of
Okhotsk

NORTH
PACIFIC
OCEAN

CYPRUS SYRIA
Mediterranean Sea LEBANON
ISRAEL
JORDAN KUWAIT

IRAQ

IRAN

AFGHANISTAN

NORTH
KOREA
SOUTH
KOREA

Sea of
Japan

JAPAN

LIBYA

EGYPT

BAHRAIN
SAUDI
Red ARABIA
Sea

Persian
Gulf
QATAR
UNITED
ARAB
EMIRATES
OMAN

PAKISTAN

Arabian
Sea

CHINA

NEPAL
BHUTAN

INDIA
BANGLADESH
MYANMAR
LAOS

HONG
KONG

TAIWAN

East
China
Sea

VOLCANO
ISLANDS

DAITO
ISLANDS
(JAPAN)

PARECE
VELA
(JAPAN)

WAKE ISLAND
(US)

⑤

CHAD

RICA SUDAN

ERITREA
YEMEN

DJIBOUTI SOMALIA

SOCOTRA
(YEMEN)

ANDAMAN
ISLANDS
(INDIA)

NICOBAR
ISLANDS
(INDIA)

THAILAND
VIETNAM
CAMBODIA

HAINAN

South
China
Sea

PHILIPPINES

Philippine
Sea

YAP
ISLANDS

NORTHERN
MARIANA
ISLANDS
(US)

GUAM
(US)

MARSHALL
ISLANDS

CENTRAL
AFRICAN
REPUBLIC
ROON

ETHIOPIA

UGANDA
KENYA

MALDIVE
ISLANDS

SRI
LANKA

BRUNEI
MALAYSIA
SINGAPORE

PALAU

FEDERATED STATE
OF MICRONESIA

NGO
DEMOCRATIC
REPUBLIC
OF THE
CONGO

RWANDA
BURUNDI
TANZANIA
ZANZIBAR

SEYCHELLES

CHAGOS ARCHIPELAGO

SUMATRA
BORNEO

CELEBES

NEW GUINEA
PAPUA
NEW
GUINEA

NAURU

KIRIBATI

SOLOMON
ISLANDS

ANGOLA

ZAMBIA MALAWI

COMOROS

INDIAN
OCEAN

JAVA

INDONESIA

TUVALU

VANUATU

MOZAMBIQUE

AMIBIA
ZIMBABWE

BOTSWANA

MADAGASCAR

MAURITIUS

Coral
Sea

CORAL SEA
ISLANDS
TERRITORY
(AUSTRALIA)

NEW
CALEDONIA

FIJI

SOUTH
PACIFIC
OCEAN

SWAZILAND

LESOTHO
SOUTH
AFRICA

⑥ AUSTRALIA

NORTH
ISLAND

NEW
ZEALAND

SOUTH
ISLAND

ICELAND

NORWAY

FINLAND

SWEDEN

North
Sea

DENMARK
NETHER-
LANDS

Baltic
Sea

ESTONIA

RUSSIA

LATVIA
LITHUANIA
RUSSIA

IRELAND
UNITED
KINGDOM

GERMANY

BELARUS

TASMANIA
(AUSTRALIA)

BELGIUM
LUXEMBOURG
LIECHTENSTEIN
SWITZER-
LAND

POLAND

CZECH
REPUBLIC
AUSTRIA SLOVAKIA

SLOVENIA

UKRAINE

MOLDOVA

UTHERN
OCEAN

FRANCE

HUNGARY
CROATIA
BOSNIA-
HERZEGOVINA

ROMANIA
SERBIA

ANDORRA

CORSICA
(FR)
MONACO
MONTENEGRO
ITALY

BULGARIA Black Sea

MACEDONIA
ALBANIA

SPAIN

PORTUGAL

SARDINIA
(IT)

BALEARIC
ISLANDS
(SP)

SICILY (IT)

GREECE

MALTA

CRETE

CYPRUS

ANTARCTICA ⑦

Mediterranean Sea

3. Europe   5. Africa   7. Antarctica

4. Asia   6. Australia

Energy and the Environment

Energy resources

1. solar energy

2. wind

3. natural gas

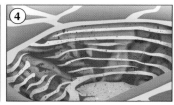

4. coal

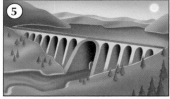

5. hydroelectric power

6. oil/petroleum

7. geothermal energy

8. nuclear energy

Pollution

9. hazardous waste

10. air pollution/smog

11. acid rain

12. water pollution

13. radiation

14. pesticide

15. oil spill

Conservation

A. recycle

B. **save** water/**conserve** water

C. **save** energy/**conserve** energy

Share your answers.

1. How do you heat your home?

2. Do you have a gas stove or an electric stove?

3. What are some ways you can save energy when it's cold?

4. Do you recycle? What products do you recycle?

5. Does your mall have recycling bins?

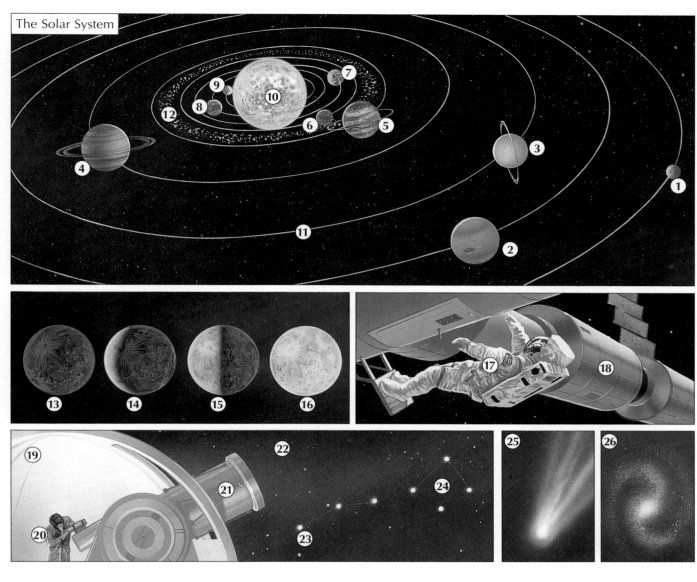

The Solar System

The planets

1. Pluto

2. Neptune

3. Uranus

4. Saturn

5. Jupiter

6. Mars

7. Earth

8. Venus

9. Mercury

10. sun

11. orbit

12. asteroid belt

13. new moon

14. crescent moon

15. quarter moon

16. full moon

17. astronaut

18. space station

19. observatory

20. astronomer

21. telescope

22. space

23. star

24. constellation

25. comet

26. galaxy

More vocabulary

lunar eclipse: when the earth is between the sun and the moon

solar eclipse: when the moon is between the earth and the sun

Share your answers.

1. Do you know the names of any constellations?

2. How do you feel when you look up at the night sky?

3. Is the night sky in Canada the same as in your country?

Trees and Plants

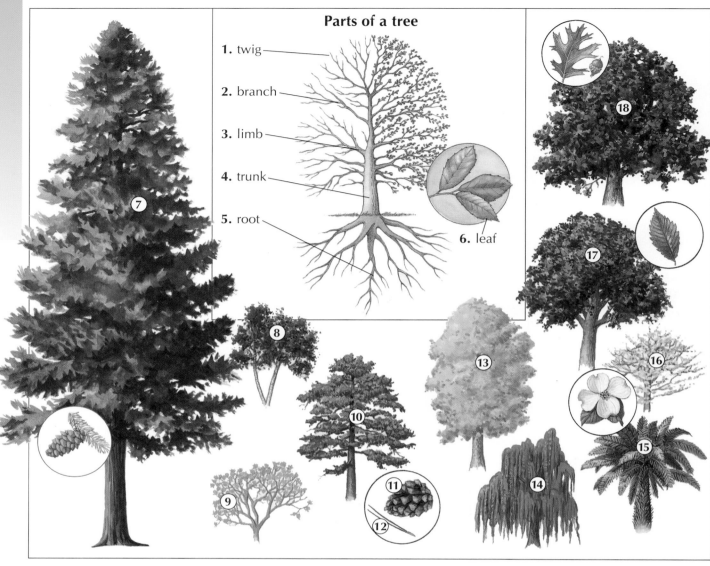

Parts of a tree

1. twig
2. branch
3. limb
4. trunk
5. root
6. leaf

7. spruce
8. birch
9. magnolia

10. pine
11. pinecone
12. needle

13. maple
14. willow
15. palm

16. dogwood
17. elm
18. oak

Plants

19. holly
20. berries

21. cactus
22. vine

23. poison oak
24. poison sumac

25. poison ivy

Parts of a flower

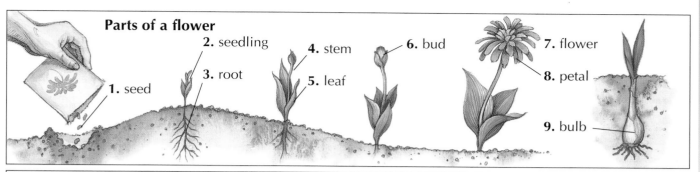

1. seed
2. seedling
3. root
4. stem
5. leaf
6. bud
7. flower
8. petal
9. bulb

10. sunflower	**15.** rose	**20.** iris	**25.** crocus
11. tulip	**16.** gardenia	**21.** jasmine	**26.** daffodil
12. hibiscus	**17.** orchid	**22.** violet	**27.** bouquet
13. marigold	**18.** carnation	**23.** poinsettia	**28.** thorn
14. daisy	**19.** chrysanthemum	**24.** lily	**29.** house plant

Marine Life, Amphibians, and Reptiles

Parts of a fish

1. fin
2. gills
3. scales

Sea animals

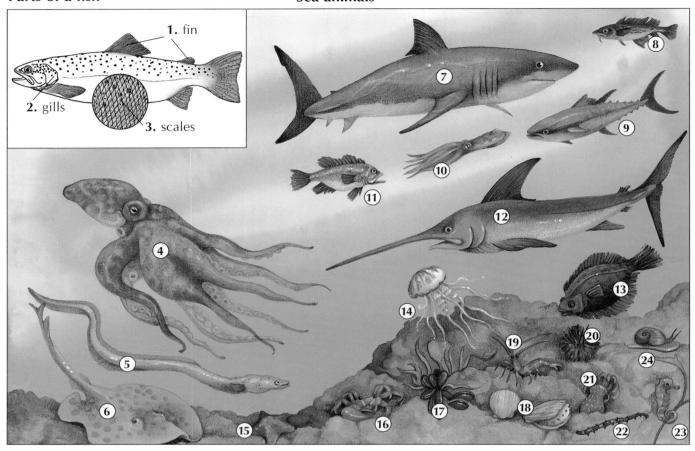

4. octopus	**11.** bass	**18.** scallop
5. eel	**12.** swordfish	**19.** shrimp
6. ray	**13.** flounder	**20.** sea urchin
7. shark	**14.** jellyfish	**21.** sea anemone
8. cod	**15.** starfish	**22.** worm
9. tuna	**16.** crab	**23.** sea horse
10. squid	**17.** mussel	**24.** snail

Amphibians

25. frog   **26.** newt   **27.** salamander   **28.** toad

Sea mammals

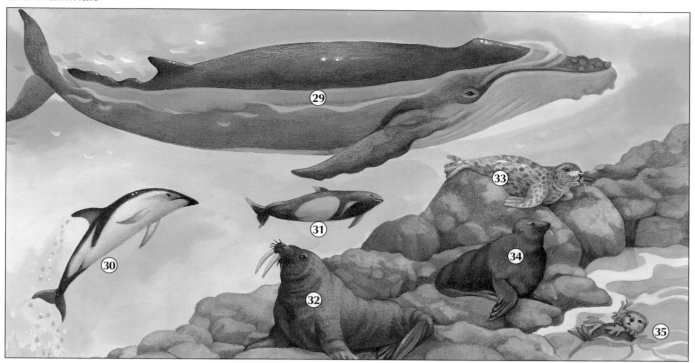

29. whale	**31.** porpoise	**33.** seal	**35.** otter
30. dolphin	**32.** walrus	**34.** sea lion	

Reptiles

36. alligator	**38.** rattlesnake	**40.** cobra	**42.** turtle
37. crocodile	**39.** garter snake	**41.** lizard	

Birds, Insects, and Arachnids

Parts of a bird

1. beak/bill
2. wing
3. nest
4. claw
5. feather

6. owl	9. woodpecker	12. penguin	15. peacock
7. blue jay	10. eagle	13. duck	16. pigeon
8. sparrow	11. hummingbird	14. goose	17. robin

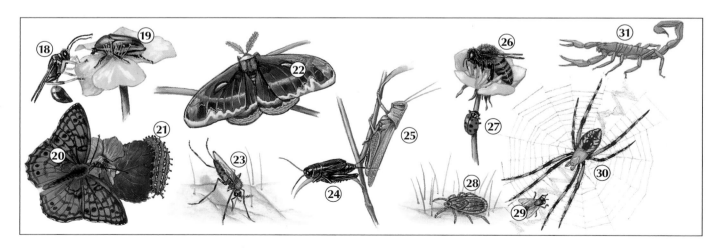

18. wasp	22. moth	26. honeybee	30. spider
19. beetle	23. mosquito	27. ladybug	31. scorpion
20. butterfly	24. cricket	28. tick	
21. caterpillar	25. grasshopper	29. fly	

Farm animals

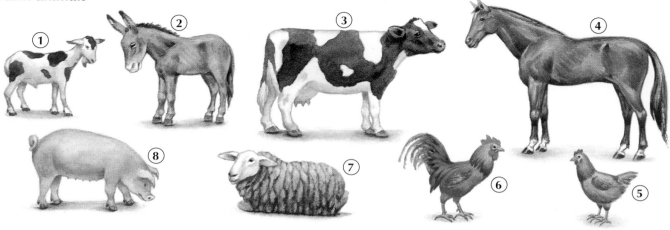

1. goat

2. donkey

3. cow

4. horse

5. hen

6. rooster

7. sheep

8. pig

Pets

9. cat

10. kitten

11. dog

12. puppy

13. rabbit

14. guinea pig

15. parakeet

16. goldfish

Rodents

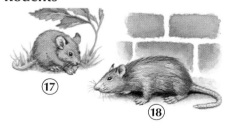

17. mouse

18. rat

19. groundhog

20. chipmunk

21. squirrel

22. prairie dog

More vocabulary

Wild animals live, eat, and raise their young away from people, in the forests, mountains, plains, etc.

Domesticated animals work for people or live with them.

Share your answers.

1. Do you have any pets? any farm animals?
2. Which of these animals are in your neighbourhood? Which are not?

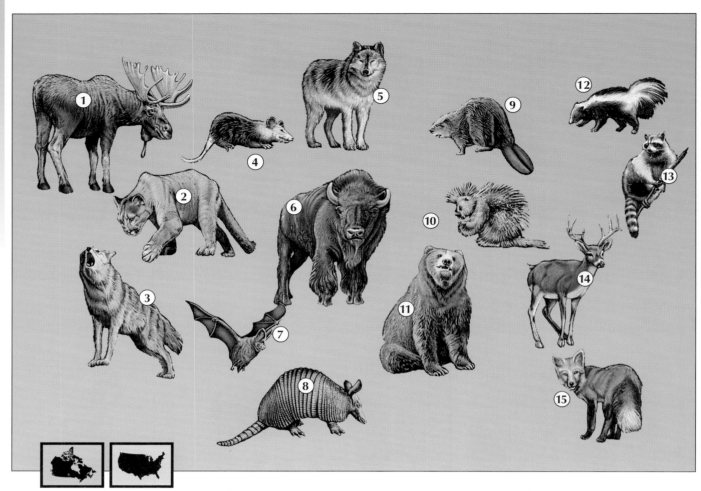

1. moose

2. mountain lion/cougar

3. coyote

4. opossum

5. wolf

6. buffalo/bison

7. bat

8. armadillo

9. beaver

10. porcupine

11. bear

12. skunk

13. raccoon

14. deer

15. fox

16. antler

17. hoof

18. whiskers

19. coat/fur

20. paw

21. horn

22. tail

23. quill

24. anteater	**30.** gorilla	**36.** lion	**42.** elephant
25. leopard	**31.** hyena	**37.** tiger	**43.** hippopotamus
26. llama	**32.** baboon	**38.** camel	**44.** kangaroo
27. monkey	**33.** giraffe	**39.** panther	**45.** koala
28. chimpanzee	**34.** zebra	**40.** orangutan	**46.** platypus
29. rhinoceros	**35.** antelope	**41.** panda	

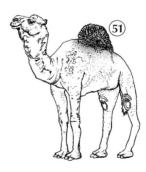

47. trunk   **48.** tusk   **49.** mane   **50.** pouch   **51.** hump

Jobs and Occupations, A–H

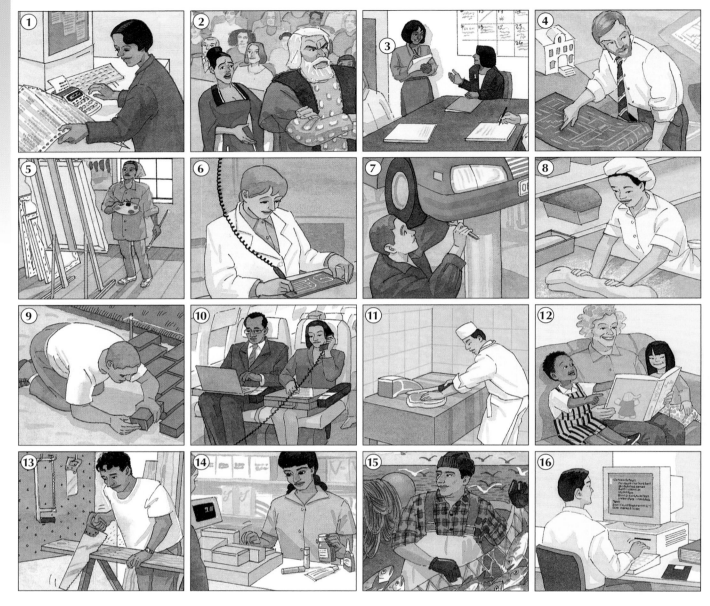

1. accountant

2. actor

3. administrative assistant

4. architect

5. artist

6. assembler

7. auto mechanic

8. baker

9. bricklayer

10. businessman/businesswoman

11. butcher

12. caregiver/babysitter

13. carpenter

14. cashier

15. commercial fisher

16. computer programmer

Use the new language.
1. Who works outside?
2. Who works inside?
3. Who makes things?

4. Who uses a computer?
5. Who wears a uniform?
6. Who sells things?

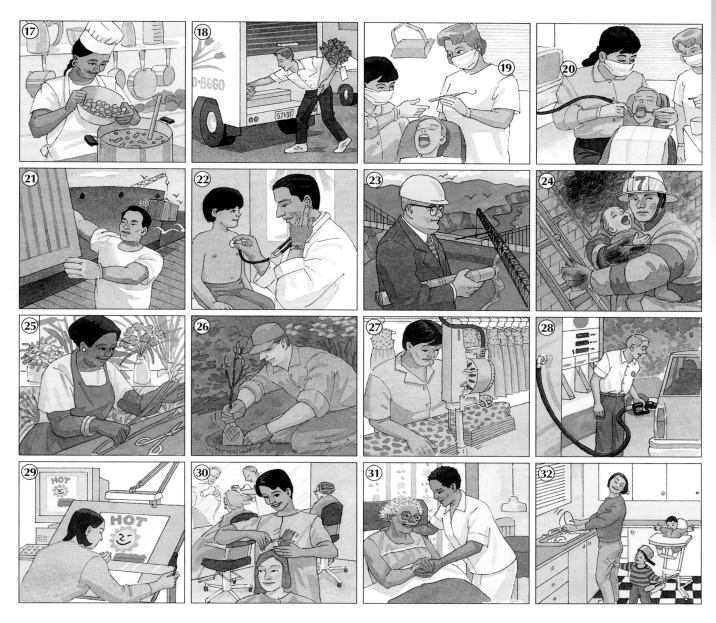

17. cook

18. delivery person

19. dental assistant

20. dentist

21. dockworker

22. doctor

23. engineer

24. firefighter

25. florist

26. gardener

27. garment worker

28. gas station attendant

29. graphic artist

30. hairdresser

31. homecare worker

32. homemaker

Share your answers.

1. Do you know people who have some of these jobs? What do they say about their work?

2. Which of these jobs are available in your city?

3. For which of these jobs do you need special training?

33. housekeeper

34. interpreter/translator

35. janitor/custodian

36. lawyer

37. machine operator

38. messenger/courier

39. model

40. mover

41. musician

42. nurse

43. painter

44. police officer

45. postal worker

46. printer

47. receptionist

48. repair person

Talk about each of the jobs or occupations.

She's a housekeeper. She works in a hotel.
He's an interpreter. He works for the government.

She's a nurse. She works with patients.

49. reporter	**55.** stock clerk	**61.** truck driver
50. salesclerk / salesperson	**56.** store owner	**62.** veterinarian
51. sanitation worker	**57.** student	**63.** welder
52. secretary	**58.** teacher / instructor	**64.** writer / author
53. server / waiter / waitress	**59.** telemarketer	
54. serviceman / servicewoman	**60.** travel agent	

Talk about your job or the job you want.

What do you do?

   I'm <u>a salesclerk.</u> I work in <u>a store.</u>

What do you want to do?

   I want to be <u>a veterinarian</u>. I want to work with <u>animals</u>.

Job Skills

A. **assemble** components	**G.** **repair** appliances	**M.** **type**
B. **assist** medical patients	**H.** **sell** cars	**N.** **use** a cash register
C. **cook**	**I.** **sew** clothes	**O.** **wait on** customers
D. **do** manual labour	**J.** **speak** another language	**P.** **work** on a computer
E. **drive** a truck	**K.** **supervise** people	
F. **operate** heavy machinery	**L.** **take care** of children	

More vocabulary

act: to perform in a play, movie, or TV show
fly: to pilot an airplane
teach: to instruct, to show how to do something

Share your answers.

1. What job skills do you have? Where did you learn them?
2. What job skills do you want to learn?

A. talk to friends

B. look at a job board

C. look for a help wanted sign

D. look in the classifieds

E. call for information

F. ask about the hours

G. fill out an application

H. go to an interview

I. talk about your experience

J. ask about benefits

K. inquire about the salary

L. get hired

An Office

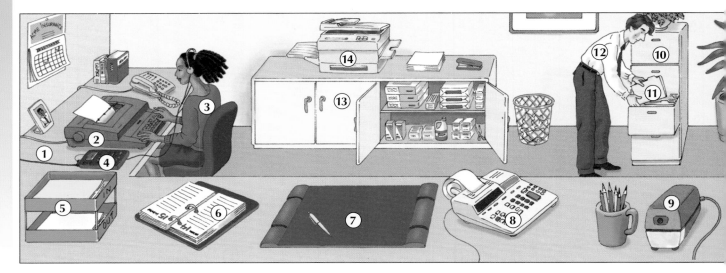

1. desk
2. typewriter
3. executive assistant
4. microcassette transcriber / dictaphone
5. stacking tray

6. desk calendar
7. desk pad
8. calculator
9. electric pencil sharpener
10. file cabinet

11. file folder
12. file clerk
13. supply cabinet
14. photocopier

A. **take** a message
B. **fax** a letter
C. **transcribe** notes

D. **type** a letter
E. **make** copies
F. **collate** papers

G. **staple**
H. **file** papers

Practise taking messages.

Hello. My name is <u>Sara Scott</u>. Is <u>Mr. Lee</u> in?
  Not yet. Would you like to leave a message?
Yes. Please ask <u>him</u> to call me at <u>555-4859</u>.

Share your answers.

1. Which office equipment do you know how to use?
2. Which jobs does a file clerk do?
3. Which jobs does an executive assistant do?

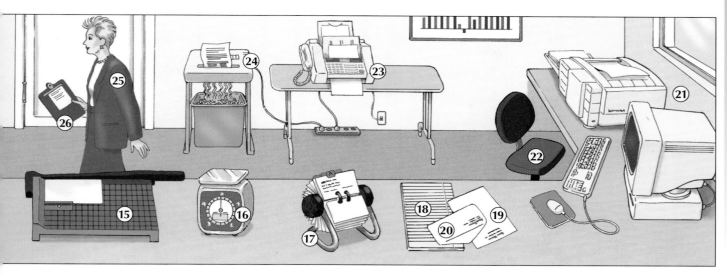

15. paper cutter

16. postal scale

17. rotary card file

18. legal pad

19. letterhead paper

20. envelope

21. computer workstation

22. swivel chair

23. fax machine

24. paper shredder

25. office manager

26. clipboard

27. appointment book

28. stapler

29. staple

30. organizer

31. typewriter cartridge

32. padded envelope

33. correction fluid

34. Post-it notes

35. label

36. notepad

37. glue

38. rubber cement

39. clear tape

40. rubber stamp

41. ink pad

42. packing tape

43. pushpin/tack

44. paper clip

45. rubber band/elastic

Use the new language.

1. Which items keep things together?

2. Which items are used to mail packages?

3. Which items are made of paper?

Share your answers.

1. Which office supplies do students use?

2. Where can you buy them?

Computers

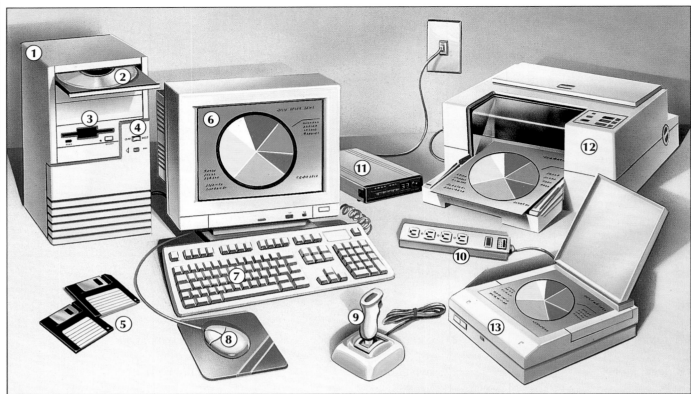

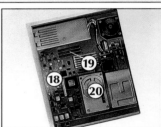

Hardware

1. CPU (central processing unit)

2. CD-ROM

3. disk drive

4. power switch

5. disk/floppy

6. monitor/screen

7. keyboard

8. mouse

9. joystick

10. surge protector/power bar

11. modem

12. printer

13. scanner

14. laptop

15. trackball

16. cable

17. port

18. motherboard

19. slot

20. hard disk drive

Software

21. program/application

22. user's manual

More vocabulary

data: information that a computer can read

memory: how much data a computer can hold

speed: how fast a computer can work with data

Share your answers.

1. Can you use a computer?

2. How did you learn? in school? from a book? by yourself?

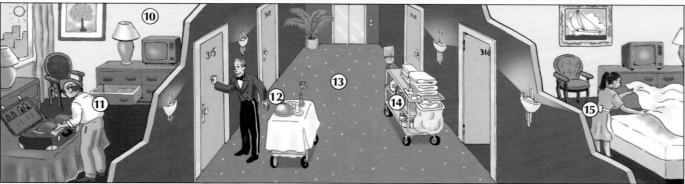

1. valet parking
2. doorman
3. lobby
4. bell captain
5. bellhop
6. luggage cart
7. gift shop

8. front desk
9. desk clerk
10. guest room
11. guest
12. room service
13. hall
14. housekeeping cart

15. housekeeper
16. pool
17. pool service
18. ice machine
19. meeting room
20. ballroom

More vocabulary

concierge: the hotel worker who helps guests find restaurants and interesting places to go

service elevator: an elevator for hotel workers

Share your answers.

1. Does this look like a hotel in your city? Which one?
2. Which hotel job is the most difficult?
3. How much does it cost to stay in a hotel in your city?

A Factory

1. front office
2. factory owner
3. designer
4. time clock
5. line supervisor
6. factory worker

7. parts
8. assembly line
9. warehouse
10. order picker
11. hand truck
12. conveyor belt

13. packer
14. forklift
15. shipping clerk
16. loading dock

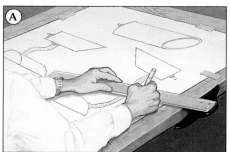

A. design

B. manufacture

C. ship

146

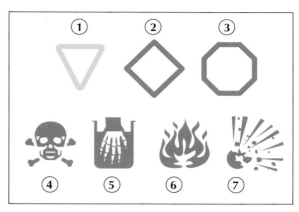  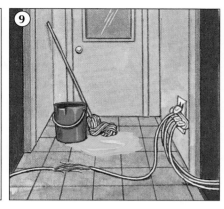

1. caution

2. warning

3. danger

4. poison

5. corrosive

6. flammable

7. explosive

8. hazardous materials

9. dangerous situation

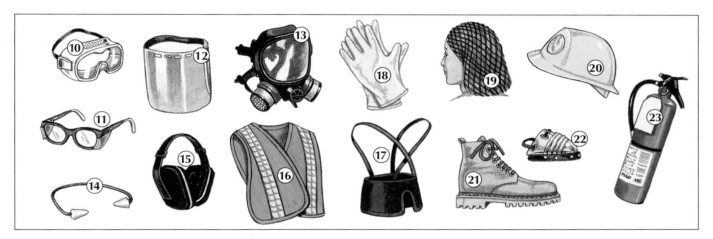

10. safety goggles

11. safety glasses

12. safety visor

13. respirator

14. earplugs

15. safety earmuffs

16. safety vest

17. back support

18. latex gloves

19. hair net

20. hard hat

21. safety boot

22. toe guard

23. fire extinguisher

24. careless

25. careful

Crops

1. rice	**8.** farmworker	**15.** farmer / grower	**22.** rancher
2. wheat	**9.** tractor	**16.** orchard	**A. plant**
3. soybeans	**10.** farm equipment	**17.** corral	**B. harvest**
4. corn	**11.** barn	**18.** hay	**C. milk**
5. alfalfa	**12.** vegetable garden	**19.** fence	**D. feed**
6. cotton	**13.** livestock	**20.** hired hand	
7. field	**14.** vineyard	**21.** steers / cattle	

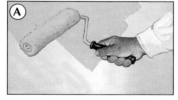   

1. construction worker

2. ladder

3. I beam/girder

4. scaffolding

5. cherry picker

6. bulldozer

7. crane

8. backhoe

9. jackhammer/pneumatic drill

10. concrete

11. bricks

12. trowel

13. insulation

14. stucco

15. window pane

16. plywood

17. wood/lumber

18. drywall

19. shingles

20. pickaxe

21. shovel

22. sledgehammer

A. **paint**

B. **lay** bricks

C. **measure**

D. **hammer**

Tools and Building Supplies

1. hammer	**4.** handsaw	**7.** pliers	**10.** circular saw
2. mallet	**5.** hacksaw	**8.** electric drill	**11.** blade
3. axe	**6.** C-clamp	**9.** power sander	**12.** router

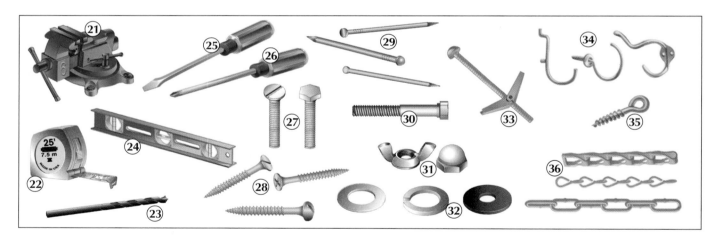

21. vise	**25.** screwdriver	**29.** nail	**33.** toggle bolt
22. tape measure	**26.** Phillips screwdriver	**30.** bolt	**34.** hook
23. drill bit	**27.** machine screw	**31.** nut	**35.** eye hook
24. level	**28.** wood screw	**32.** washer	**36.** chain

Use the new language.

1. Which tools are used for plumbing?
2. Which tools are used for painting?

3. Which tools are used for electrical work?
4. Which tools are used for working with wood?

13. wire

14. extension cord

15. metrestick

16. pipe

17. fittings

18. wood

19. spray gun

20. paint

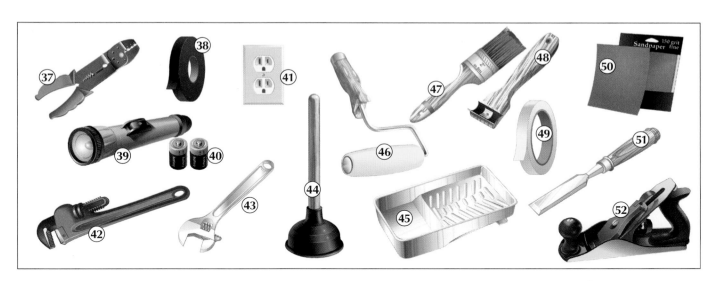

37. wire stripper

38. electrical tape

39. flashlight

40. battery

41. outlet

42. pipe wrench

43. wrench

44. plunger

45. paint pan

46. paint roller

47. paintbrush

48. scraper

49. masking tape

50. sandpaper

51. chisel

52. plane

Use the new language.

Look at **Household Problems and Repairs,** pages **48–49.**

Name the tools you use to fix the problems you see.

Share your answers.

1. Which tools do you have in your home?

2. Which tools can be dangerous to use?

Places to Go

1. zoo	**10.** the movies	**19.** fair/exhibition
2. animals	**11.** seat	**20.** first place/first prize
3. zookeeper	**12.** screen	**21.** art exhibition
4. botanical gardens	**13.** amusement park	**22.** flea market
5. greenhouse	**14.** puppet show	**23.** booth
6. gardener	**15.** roller coaster	**24.** merchandise
7. art gallery	**16.** carnival	**25.** baseball game
8. painting	**17.** rides	**26.** stadium
9. sculpture	**18.** game	**27.** announcer

Talk about the places you like to go.

I like <u>animals</u>, so I go to <u>the zoo</u>.
I like <u>rides</u>, so I go to <u>carnivals</u>.

Share your answers.

1. Which of these places is interesting to you?
2. Which rides do you like at an amusement park?
3. What are some famous places to go to in your country?

1. ball field

2. bike path

3. cyclist

4. bicycle/bike

5. jump rope/skipping rope

6. duck pond

7. tennis court

8. picnic table

9. tricycle

10. bench

11. water fountain

12. swings

13. slide

14. climbing apparatus

15. sandbox

16. seesaw

A. **pull** the wagon

B. **push** the swing

C. **climb** on the bars

D. **picnic/have** a picnic

Outdoor Recreation

1. camping

2. boating

3. canoeing

4. rafting

5. fishing

6. hiking

7. backpacking

8. mountain biking

9. horseback riding

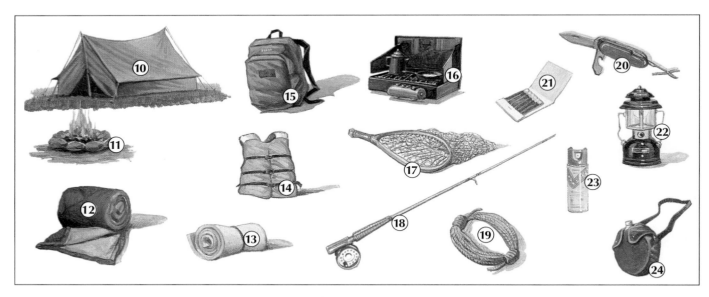

10. tent

11. campfire

12. sleeping bag

13. foam pad

14. life vest

15. backpack

16. camping stove

17. fishing net

18. fishing rod

19. rope

20. multi-use knife

21. matches

22. lantern

23. insect repellent

24. canteen

1. ocean/water	**10.** sand castle	**19.** lifesaving device
2. fins	**11.** cooler	**20.** lifeguard station
3. diving mask	**12.** shade	**21.** seashell
4. sailboat	**13.** sunscreen/sunblock	**22.** pail/bucket
5. surfboard	**14.** beach chair	**23.** sand
6. wave	**15.** beach towel	**24.** rock
7. wet suit	**16.** pier	
8. scuba tank	**17.** sunbather	
9. beach umbrella	**18.** lifeguard	

More vocabulary

seaweed: a plant that grows in the ocean

tide: the level of the ocean. The tide goes in and out every twelve hours.

Share your answers.

1. Are there any beaches near your home?
2. Do you prefer to spend more time on the sand or in the water?
3. Where are some of the world's best beaches?

Sports Verbs

A. walk

B. jog

C. run

D. throw

E. catch

F. pitch

G. hit

H. pass

I. shoot

J. jump

K. dribble / bounce

L. kick

M. tackle

Practise talking about what you can do.
I can <u>swim</u>, but I can't <u>dive</u>.
I can <u>pass the ball</u> well, but I can't <u>shoot</u> too well.

Use the new language.
Look at **Individual Sports,** page **159.**
Name the actions you see people doing.
The man in number 18 is riding a horse.

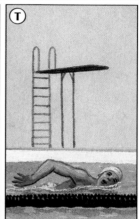

FINISH

N. serve

O. swing

P. exercise / work out

Q. stretch

R. bend

S. dive

T. swim

U. ski

V. rollerblade™

W. ride

X. start

Y. race

Z. finish

Share your answers.

1. What do you like to do?
2. What do you have difficulty doing?

3. How often do you exercise? Once a week? Two or three times a week? More? Never?
4. Which is more difficult, throwing a ball or catching it?

Team Sports

Hockey

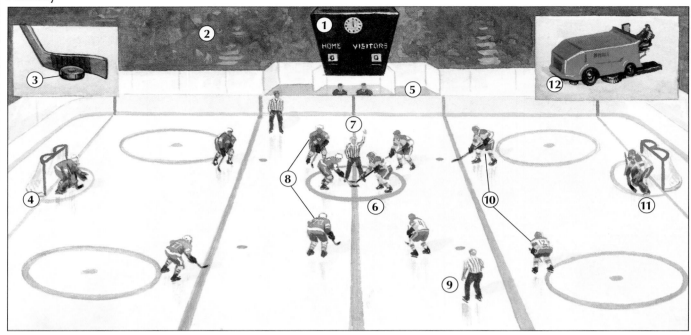

1. scoreboard	**4.** net	**7.** referee	**10.** defence
2. fans	**5.** penalty box	**8.** forwards	**11.** goalie
3. puck	**6.** face off circle	**9.** linesman	**12.** ice resurfacing machine (Zamboni™)

13. basketball	**16.** football	**19.** volleyball
14. baseball	**17.** soccer	**20.** lacrosse
15. softball	**18.** curling	

More vocabulary

captain: the team leader

umpire: in baseball, the name for the referee

Little League: a baseball league for children

win: to have the best score

lose: the opposite of win

tie: to have the same score as the other team

1. archery

2. billiards/pool

3. bowling

4. cycling/biking

5. fencing

6. flying disc*

7. golf

8. gymnastics

9. inline skating

10. martial arts

11. racquetball

12. skateboarding

13. table tennis/ Ping-Pong™

14. tennis

15. weightlifting

16. wrestling

17. track and field

18. horse racing

*Note: One brand is Frisbee® (Mattel, Inc.)

Talk about sports.

Which sports do you like?

I like tennis but I don't like golf.

Share your answers.

1. Which sports are good for children to learn? Why?
2. Which sport is the most difficult to learn? Why?
3. Which sport is the most dangerous? Why?

Winter Sports and Water Sports

1. downhill skiing

2. snowboarding

3. cross-country skiing

4. snowmobiling

5. skating/figure skating

6. sledding/tobogganing

7. waterskiing

8. sailing

9. surfing

10. sailboarding/windsurfing

11. snorkelling

12. scuba diving

Use the new language.
Look at **The Beach,** page 155.
Name the sports you see.

Share your answers.
1. Which sports are in the Winter Olympics?
2. Which sports do you think are the most exciting to watch?

1. golf club	**8.** target	**15.** catcher's mask	**22.** football
2. tennis racquet	**9.** ice skates	**16.** uniform	**23.** snowboard
3. volleyball	**10.** inline skates	**17.** glove	**24.** skis
4. basketball	**11.** hockey stick	**18.** baseball	**25.** ski poles
5. bowling ball	**12.** soccer ball	**19.** weights	**26.** ski boots
6. bow	**13.** shin guards	**20.** football helmet	**27.** flying disc*
7. arrow	**14.** baseball bat	**21.** shoulder pads	***Note:** one brand is Frisbee® (Mattel, Inc.)

Share your answers.

1. Which sports equipment is used for safety reasons?
2. Which sports equipment is heavy?
3. What sports equipment do you have at home?

Use the new language.

Look at **Individual Sports,** page **159.**
Name the sports equipment you see.

Hobbies and Games

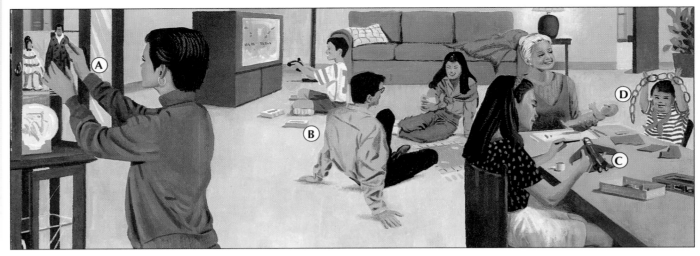

| A. **collect** things | B. **play** games | C. **build** models | D. **do** crafts |

1. video game system	5. checkers	9. acrylic paint	13. coin collection
2. cartridge	6. chess	10. figurine	14. clay
3. board game	7. model kit	11. baseball card	15. doll making kit
4. dice	8. glue	12. stamp collection	16. woodworking kit

Talk about how much time you spend on your hobbies.

I *do crafts* all the time.
I *play chess* sometimes.
I never *build models*.

Share your answers.

1. How often do you play video games? Often? Sometimes? Never?
2. What board games do you know?
3. Do you collect anything? What?

E. paint   **F. knit**   **G. pretend**   **H. play** cards

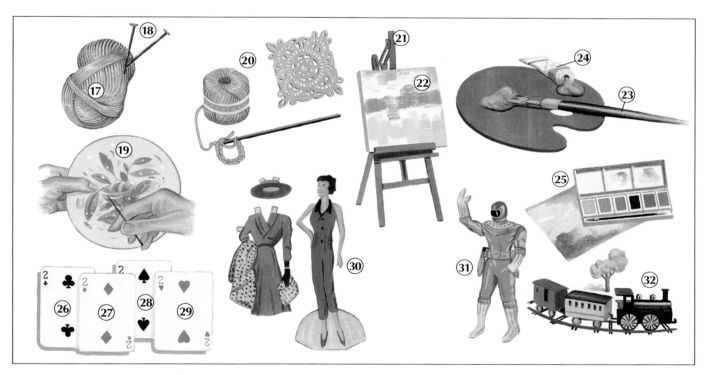

17. yarn	**21.** easel	**25.** watercolour	**29.** hearts
18. knitting needles	**22.** canvas	**26.** clubs	**30.** paper doll
19. embroidery	**23.** paintbrush	**27.** diamonds	**31.** action figure
20. crochet	**24.** oil paint	**28.** spades	**32.** model trains

Share your answers.

1. Do you like to play cards? Which games?
2. Did you pretend a lot when you were a child? What did you pretend to be?
3. Is it important to have hobbies? Why or why not?
4. What's your favourite game?
5. What's your hobby?

1. clock radio

2. portable radio-cassette player

3. cassette recorder

4. microphone

5. shortwave radio

6. TV (television)

7. portable TV

8. VCR (videocassette recorder)

9. remote control

10. videocassette/videotape

11. speakers

12. turntable

13. tuner

14. CD player

15. personal radio-cassette player

16. headphones

17. adapter

18. plug

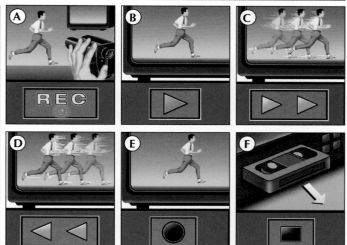

19. video camera

20. tripod

21. camcorder

22. battery pack

23. battery charger

24. 35 mm camera

25. zoom lens

26. film

27. camera case

28. screen

29. carousel slide projector

30. slide tray

31. slides

32. photo album

33. out of focus

34. overexposed

35. underexposed

A. record

B. play

C. fast forward

D. rewind

E. pause

F. stop and **eject**

Entertainment

Types of entertainment

1. film/movie

2. play

3. television program

4. radio program

5. stand-up comedy

6. concert

7. ballet

8. opera

Types of stories

9. western

10. comedy

11. tragedy

12. science fiction story

13. action story/
adventure story/thriller

14. horror story

15. mystery

16. romance

166

Types of TV programs

17. news

18. sitcom (situation comedy)

19. cartoon

20. talk show

21. soap opera

22. nature program

23. game show/quiz show

24. children's program

25. shopping program

26. serious book

27. funny book

28. sad book

29. boring book

30. interesting book

Holidays

1. New Year's Day

2. parade

3. float

4. Valentine's Day

5. card

6. heart

7. Canada Day

8. fireworks

9. flag

10. Halloween

11. jack-o'-lantern

12. mask

13. costume

14. candy

15. Thanksgiving

16. feast

17. turkey

18. Christmas

19. ornament

20. Christmas tree

Note: Many other holidays are celebrated by the various cultural groups in Canada.

A. **plan** a party

B. **invite** the guests

C. **decorate** the house

D. **wrap** a gift

E. **hide**

F. **answer** the door

G. **shout** "surprise!"

H. **light** the candles

I. **sing** "Happy Birthday"

J. **make** a wish

K. **blow out** the candles

L. **open** the presents

Practise inviting friends to a party.

I'd love for you to come to my party <u>next week</u>.

Could <u>you and your friend</u> come to my party?

Would <u>your friend</u> like to come to a party I'm giving?

Share your answers.

1. Do you celebrate birthdays? What do you do?

2. Are there birthdays you celebrate in a special way?

3. Is there a special birthday song in your country?

Verb Guide

Verbs in English are either regular or irregular in the past tense and past participle forms.

Regular Verbs

The regular verbs below are marked 1, 2, 3, or 4 according to four different spelling patterns. (See page 172 for the **irregular verbs** which do not follow any of these patterns.)

Spelling Patterns for the Past and the Past Participle	*Example*		
1. Add **-ed** to the end of the verb.	**ASK**	→	**ASKED**
2. Add **-d** to the end of the verb.	**LIVE**	→	**LIVED**
3. Double the final consonant and add **-ed** to the end of the verb.	**DROP**	→	**DROPPED**
4. Drop the final y and add **-ied** to the end of the verb.	**CRY**	→	**CRIED**

The Oxford Picture Dictionary List of Regular Verbs

act (1)
add (1)
address (1)
answer (1)
apologize (2)
appear (1)
applaud (1)
arrange (2)
arrest (1)
arrive (2)
ask (1)
assemble (2)
assist (1)
bake (2)
barbecue (2)
bathe (2)
board (1)
boil (1)
borrow (1)
bounce (2)
brainstorm (1)
breathe (2)
broil (1)
brush (1)
burn (1)
call (1)
carry (4)
change (2)
check (1)
choke (2)
chop (3)
circle (2)
claim (1)
clap (3)
clean (1)
clear (1)
climb (1)
close (2)
collate (2)

collect (1)
colour (1)
comb (1)
commit (3)
compliment (1)
conserve (2)
convert (1)
cook (1)
copy (4)
correct (1)
cough (1)
count (1)
cross (1)
cry (4)
dance (2)
design (1)
deposit (1)
deliver (1)
dial (1)
dictate (2)
die (2)
discuss (1)
dive (2)
dress (1)
dribble (2)
drill (1)
drop (3)
drown (1)
dry (4)
dust (1)
dye (2)
edit (1)
eject (1)
empty (4)
end (1)
enter (1)
erase (2)
examine (2)
exchange (2)

exercise (2)
experience (2)
exterminate (2)
fasten (1)
fax (1)
file (2)
fill (1)
finish (1)
fix (1)
floss (1)
fold (1)
fry (4)
gargle (2)
graduate (2)
grate (2)
grease (2)
greet (1)
grill (1)
hail (1)
hammer (1)
harvest (1)
help (1)
hire (2)
hug (3)
immigrate (2)
inquire (2)
insert (1)
introduce (2)
invite (2)
iron (1)
jog (3)
join (1)
jump (1)
kick (1)
kiss (1)
knit (3)
land (1)
laugh (1)
learn (1)

lengthen (1)
listen (1)
live (2)
load (1)
lock (1)
look (1)
mail (1)
manufacture (2)
mark (1)
match (1)
measure (2)
milk (1)
miss (1)
mix (1)
mop (3)
move (2)
mow (1)
need (1)
nurse (2)
obey (1)
observe (2)
open (1)
operate (2)
order (1)
overdose (2)
paint (1)
park (1)
pass (1)
pause (2)
peel (1)
perm (1)
pick (1)
pitch (1)
plan (3)
plant (1)
play (1)
point (1)
polish (1)
pour (1)
pretend (1)
print (1)
protect (1)

pull (1)
push (1)
race (2)
raise (2)
rake (2)
receive (2)
record (1)
recycle (2)
register (1)
relax (1)
remove (2)
rent (1)
repair (1)
repeat (1)
report (1)
request (1)
return (1)
rinse (2)
roast (1)
rock (1)
sauté (2)
save (2)
scrub (3)
seat (1)
sentence (2)
serve (2)
share (2)
shave (2)
ship (3)
shop (3)
shorten (1)
shout (1)
sign (1)
simmer (1)
skate (2)
ski (1)
slice (2)
smell (1)
sneeze (2)
sort (1)
spell (1)
staple (2)

start (1)
stay (1)
steam (1)
stir (3)
stir-fry (4)
stop (3)
stow (1)
stretch (1)
supervise (2)
swallow (1)
tackle (2)
talk (1)
taste (2)
thank (1)
tie (2)
touch (1)
transcribe (2)
transfer (3)
travel (1)
trim (3)
turn (1)
type (2)
underline (2)
unload (1)
unpack (1)
use (2)
vacuum (1)
vomit (1)
vote (2)
wait (1)
walk (1)
wash (1)
watch (1)
water (1)
weed (1)
weigh (1)
wipe (2)
work (1)
wrap (3)
yield (1)

Irregular Verbs

These verbs have irregular endings in the past and/or the past participle.

The Oxford Picture Dictionary List of Irregular Verbs

simple	past	past participle	simple	past	past participle
be	was	been	leave	left	left
beat	beat	beaten	lend	lent	lent
become	became	become	let	let	let
begin	began	begun	light	lit	lit
bend	bent	bent	make	made	made
bleed	bled	bled	pay	paid	paid
blow	blew	blown	picnic	picnicked	picnicked
break	broke	broken	put	put	put
build	built	built	read	read	read
buy	bought	bought	rewind	rewound	rewound
catch	caught	caught	rewrite	rewrote	rewritten
come	came	come	ride	rode	ridden
cut	cut	cut	run	ran	run
do	did	done	say	said	said
draw	drew	drawn	see	saw	seen
drink	drank	drunk	sell	sold	sold
drive	drove	driven	send	sent	sent
eat	ate	eaten	set	set	set
fall	fell	fallen	sew	sewed	sewn
feed	fed	fed	shoot	shot	shot
feel	felt	felt	sing	sang	sung
find	found	found	sit	sat	sat
fly	flew	flown	speak	spoke	spoken
get	got	gotten	stand	stood	stood
give	gave	given	sweep	swept	swept
go	went	gone	swim	swam	swum
hang	hung	hung	swing	swung	swung
have	had	had	take	took	taken
hear	heard	heard	teach	taught	taught
hide	hid	hidden	throw	threw	thrown
hit	hit	hit	wake	woke	woken
hold	held	held	wear	wore	worn
keep	kept	kept	withdraw	withdrew	withdrawn
lay	laid	laid	write	wrote	written

Index

Two numbers are shown after words in the index: the first refers to the page where the word is illustrated and the second refers to the item number of the word on that page. For example, cool [ko͞ol] **10**-3 means that the word *cool* is item number 3 on page 10. If only the bold page number appears, then that word is part of the unit title or subtitle, or is found somewhere else on the page. A bold number followed by ✦ means the word can be found in the exercise space at the bottom of that page.

Words or combinations of words that appear in **bold** type are used as verbs or verb phrases. Words used as other parts of speech are shown in ordinary type. So, for example, **file** (in bold type) is the verb *file*, while file (in ordinary type) is the noun *file*. Words or phrases in small capital letters (for example, HOLIDAYS) form unit titles.

Phrases and other words that form combinations with an individual word entry are often listed underneath it. Rather than repeating the word each time it occurs in combination with what is listed under it, the word is replaced by three dots (...), called an ellipsis. For example, under the word *bus*, you will find ...driver and ...stop meaning *bus driver* and *bus stop*. Under the word *store* you will find shoe... and toy..., meaning *shoe store* and *toy store*.

Pronunciation Guide

The index includes a pronunciation guide for all the words and phrases illustrated in the book. This guide uses symbols commonly found in dictionaries for native speakers. These symbols, unlike those used in pronunciation systems such as the International Phonetic Alphabet, tend to use English spelling patterns and so should help you to become more aware of the connections between written English and spoken English.

Consonants

[b] as in back [băk]	[k] as in key [kē]	[sh] as in shoe [sho͞o]
[ch] as in cheek [chēk]	[l] as in leaf [lēf]	[t] as in tape [tāp]
[d] as in date [dāt]	[m] as in match [măch]	[th] as in three [thrē]
[dh] as in this [dhĭs]	[n] as in neck [nĕk]	[v] as in vine [vīn]
[f] as in face [fās]	[ng] as in ring [rĭng]	[w] as in wait [wāt]
[g] as in gas [găs]	[p] as in park [pärk]	[y] as in yams [yămz]
[h] as in half [hăf]	[r] as in rice [rīs]	[z] as in zoo [zo͞o]
[j] as in jam [jăm]	[s] as in sand [sănd]	[zh] as in measure [mĕzh′ər]

Vowels

[ā] as in bake [bāk]	[ĭ] as in lip [lĭp]	[ow] as in cow [kow]
[ă] as in back [băk]	[ï] as in near [nïr]	[oy] as in boy [boy]
[ä] as in car [kär]	[ō] as in cold [kōld]	[ŭ] as in cut [kŭt]
[ē] as in beat [bēt]	[ö] as in box [böks]	[ü] as in curb [kürb]
[ĕ] as in bed [bĕd]	[ö] as in short [shört]	[ə] as in above [ə bŭv′]
[ë] as in bear [bër]	[o͞o] as in cool [ko͞ol]	
[ī] as in line [līn]	[o͝o] as in cook [ko͝ok]	

All the pronunciation symbols used are alphabetical except for the schwa [ə]. The schwa is the most frequent vowel sound in English. If you use the schwa appropriately in unstressed syllables, your pronunciation will sound more natural.

Vowels before [r] are shown with the symbol [¨] to call attention to the special quality that vowels have before [r]. You should listen carefully to native speakers to discover how these vowels actually sound.

Stress

This index follows the system for marking stress used in many dictionaries for native speakers.

1. Stress is not marked if a word consisting of a single syllable occurs by itself.

2. Where stress is marked, two levels are distinguished:

a bold accent [′] is placed after each syllable with primary (or strong) stress, a light accent [′] is placed after each syllable with secondary (or weaker) stress.

In phrases and other combinations of words, stress is indicated for each word as it would be pronounced within the whole phrase or other unit. If a word consisting of a single syllable is stressed in the combinations listed below it, the accent mark indicating the degree of stress it has in the phrases (primary or secondary) is shown in parentheses. A hyphen replaces any part of a word or phrase that is omitted. For example, bus [bŭs(′–)] shows that the word *bus* is said with primary stress in the combinations shown below it. The word ...driver [–drī′vər], listed under *bus*, shows that *driver* has secondary stress in the combination *bus driver*: [bŭs′ drī′vər].

Syllable Boundaries

Syllable boundaries are indicated by a single space or by a stress mark.

Index

Index

Index

Index

Index

Index

Index

Index

Index

Index

Index

Index

Index

Index